creating art
from fibers
and fabrics

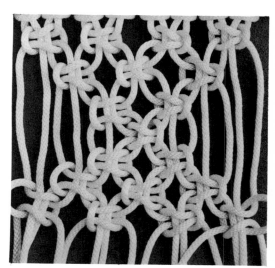

Galahad Books • New York

creating art from fibers and fabrics

Dona Z. Meilach

Published by Galahad Books, a division of A & W
Promotional Book Corporation, 95 Madison Ave-
nue, New York, N.Y. 10016, by arrangement with
Henry Regnery Company, 114 West Illinois Street,
Chicago, Ill. 60610.

Library of Congress Catalog Card No.: 73–79818
ISBN: 0–88365–041–X

Manufactured in the United States of America.

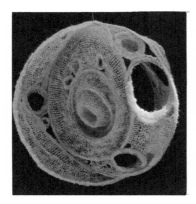

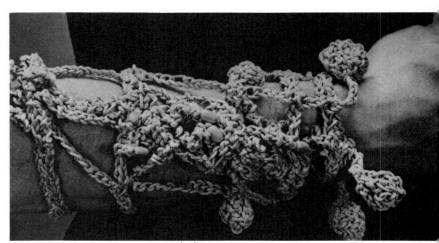

Book design by Mary MacDonald

CONTENTS

CROCHETED SCULPTURAL HANGINGS.
(Details). Jane Knight.
PHOTO: RICHARD KNIGHT

art from fibers and fabrics

Ever since man learned to spin wool into fiber and interlock fibers into fabrics he has developed methods and materials that have continued to be used by craftsmen through the centuries. Innovation, exploration, and experimentation have coaxed the arts along new, creative paths. Now modern craftsmen appear to be throwing open the door to even more inventive and imaginative uses for techniques that are centuries old.

Fibers and fabrics have been updated by modern chemical technology to the extent that there is a tremendous variety of natural and synthetic materials in a wild array of textures, colors, and content. The results are staggering in their concepts. Art made from fibers and fabrics is beginning to command almost as much attention from art collectors and museum directors as are painting and hard sculpture. Techniques such as quilting, knitting, crochet, knotting, patchwork, and weaving, which traditionally have produced utilitarian items, are now appearing in works of art that must jolt

WOODEN MASK WITH
TWISTED FIBERS.
Bella Coola Indians.
British Columbia,
Canada. Many craftsmen
study the art of primitive
cultures to stimulate
ideas for modern
statements.
*COURTESY:
SMITHSONIAN INSTITUTION,
WASHINGTON, D. C.*

us out of our complacency about the methods. For example,
crochet usually reminds us of baby booties, sweaters, shawls,
hats, and dresses. But it offers new potential for the artist when
it results in sculptural forms such as those created by Jane Knight
and Bonnie Meltzer.

The use of fibers to capture and intertwine with space is exciting
and compelling for anyone seeking new challenges. Macramé, a
knotting technique the origins of which are lost in antiquity, has
been rediscovered in the past few years. Cords, twines, strings,
and yarns of every conceivable material are emerging in new har-
monies of color, texture, and shape for hangings and sculpture
as well as for practical items. Wrapping with fibers, an offshoot of
macramé, is fascinating, and its potential is only beginning to be
explored. Padded work as it exists today could almost—but not
quite—be placed in the categories of Italian trapunto and quilting.
However, many craftsmen who are creating padded artwork have

CHRIST CARRYING THE CROSS.
Unknown German artist, c. 1750. Stitchery and appliqué were used in this early pictorial work.
COURTESY: THE COOPER UNION MUSEUM, NEW YORK

no knowledge of these old techniques; they have simply discovered a vehicle for a statement that expresses today's environment and ideas.

Fabrics are often combined with materials of the painter, such as acrylics, oils, and water colors. With the development of efficient glues and polymers, fabrics and fibers have become a marvelous medium for the collage artist to explore. Collage—first associated with pasted papers and sometimes with woven materials on a flat surface—now encompasses a variety of materials in many playful and serious two- and three-dimensional arrangements. Collage is also combined with appliqué, a traditional needlework approach to pictorial fabric usage. It is interesting to note that appliqué is no longer the tightly turned-under hem method that was sewn with tiny stitches so charmingly and painstakingly by our early American ancestors. Today appliqué may be used to explore the contrast of textures and to juxtapose rough and smooth

HANGING.
Student. Design West, Los Angeles.
The ability to use many techniques
to make one statement is illustrated
in this combined rug hooking,
wrapping, and weaving.

HANGING.
Virginia Tiffany. Macramé
knotting. Jute. The artist has
worked an assymetrical design
from a piece of old wood.
PHOTOGRAPHED AT ART INDEPENDENT,
LAKE GENEVA, WISCONSIN

fabrics and shaggy edges and to capture a spirit that seems to
reflect the essence of the times.

No longer do you see hooked rugs exhibiting traditional designs
with tightly controlled patterns and even surfaces. Today's rugs
are often found hanging on walls just as they hung in ancient
Scandinavian countries, but now they are not meant for insulation
against the cold; rather, they are hung as paintings. Yarn textures
such as wool, synthetics, horsehair, sisal, and items including
bird feathers, shells, and leather strips often are worked into a
brilliant, rich, highly tactile surface. Fibers may hang several
inches from the background, and colors and designs are as wild as
an abstract expressionist's canvas. Traute Ishida mounts her rugs
on wood and makes these free-form shapes wrap into corners, onto
ceilings, or partly on a floor. Efficient rug-making instruments are
partly responsible for the new approach to textiles. Learning to use
these devices is simple, and the work progresses quickly.

6

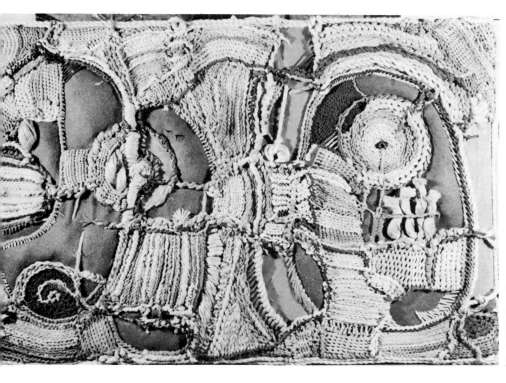

MASKS.
Ruben Steinberg.
Rope knotting and
padded leather
bundles are made
from World War I
army blankets.

Why are fibers and fabrics becoming increasingly appealing to
artists? Most artists agree that because the materials are so varied,
the expressive and decorative possibilities are unlimited. Soft and
flexible materials allow you to create a new kind of sculpture,
one that you can't achieve with wood, stone, or metal. Because
we all are so familiar with fabrics in our daily lives, we react to
them personally, through their appeal to our visual and tactile
senses. An additional bonus is that no complicated equipment and
work space are necessary in working with fibers and fabrics. And
there is no mess, as there sometimes is with other art media.

Creating art from fibers and fabrics may be approached in
several ways. Some artists who are at home with a technique such
as macramé or knitting, for examples, will think of a form that
they can achieve and then will seek the material for creating that
form. Others will have materials on hand, think about them,
and manipulate them until the materials suggest the form.

CAPE WITH HANDS.
Sas Colby. Padded
work and appliqué.
COURTESY: ARTIST

Ideally, however, you should be able to visualize or work toward a form and become familiar with many materials and methods that can help you to achieve the results you want. If a form requires that you learn a new technique, by all means learn it. The search for new materials should be never ending.

Examples throughout the book show several techniques and materials that have been combined to give dramatic impact. It is the ability to move freely from one technique to another, to combine materials, and to evolve statements unfettered by traditional approaches that is creating the unprecedented explosion of art from fibers and fabrics.

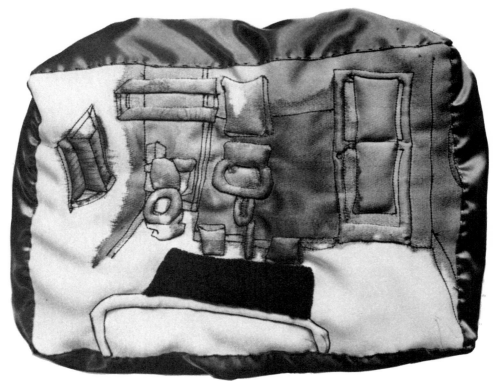

BATHROOM SCENE.
Linda Vetter. The fabric was painted to depict the scene and then was stitched by machine. Stuffing was added to give the painting dimension. This technique is a modern version of Italian trapunto. The finished piece was made into a soft pillow form.

FIBER SCULPTURE.
Kumiko Murashima. Nylon hooked through a shaped piece of screen wire.

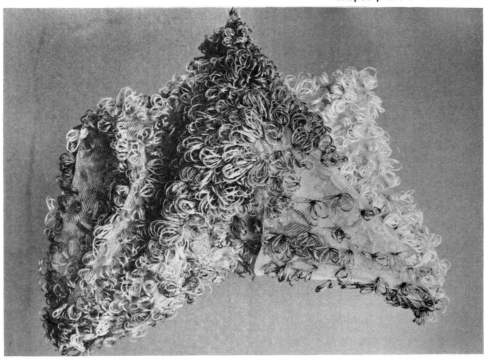

FIBER FALL.
(Detail). Terry Illes. Horsehair wrapped with
purple Persian wool and rust-colored silk.

PHOTO: DAVE REPP

wrapping

Wrapping is rapidly becoming a popular technique for a variety of fiber hangings and sculptures. The method is simple; lengths of fibers are wrapped around multiples of other fibers in various diameters, colors, and textures. Wrapping probably originated with the belts and yarn work of the Peruvian Indians; one of the wrapping techniques illustrated in this chapter is derived from that source.

Weavers have frequently employed wrapping techniques to bundle groups of warp threads. More recently wrapping has become extremely popular as an adjunct to the knots of macramé. Wrapping provides a neat finish for loose ends of multiple cords. It also may be used within a series of knotted cords to create a change of design. Perhaps the practice of wrapping in macramé has prompted artists to pursue its potential as an independent and separate technique—the results are continually innovative and exciting.

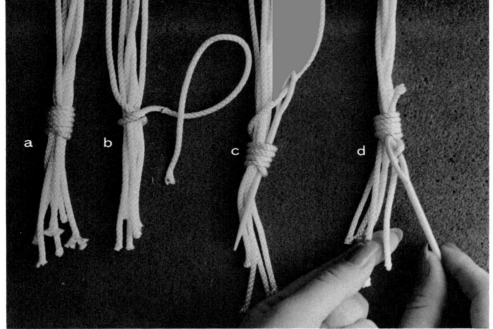

NEEDLE WRAPPING.

(a) A finished coil may be wrapped with one of the cords from a grouping, or a new cord may be introduced. Any multiple may be used. A large-eye rug, weaving, or tapestry needle or a piece of bent wire may be used for the wrapping.

(b) With the end of one cord begin wrapping from the bottom of the coil. Overlap the first wrap to prevent the coil from slipping; then continue winding.

(c) Place a large-eye needle into the coil with the eye of the needle at the top. At the end of the number of wraps desired, thread the loose end of the coil through the eye of the needle.

(d) Pull the needle through all the wraps to the bottom of the coil. Tighten the coil by twisting the needle gently. The end of the coil may be cut close, and a dab of white glue may be placed at the end to hold it secure. For cords that are too thick to thread through a needle, wrap them loosely and push the end of the cord back down through the wraps and tighten. Wrapping also may be done from top to bottom by wrapping the cord in with the eye of the needle at the bottom of the coil, then lacing and pulling the cord up.

The examples of wrapping shown here illustrate the versatility of the technique used alone or in combination with other methods. In Esther Robinson's hanging (page 14) you will notice that wrapping has been used to create a shape as well as to provide a space between other fibers. Wrapping brown jute around natural sisal combined with macramé is a way of achieving three-dimensional sculpture without using hard wire or a wood armature (see the piece by Dona Meilach on page 15). Evelyn Svec Ward has used heavy fibers as a core and wrapped them to create free-standing sculptures.

Fibers of any kind may be used for wrapping—hemp, sisal, manila, synthetic fibers, yarns, horsehair, mohair, goat hair yarn, and whatever else is available. Many kinds of ordinary rope and heavy twines may be purchased from your local hardware store. The more exotic fibers can be ordered readily from sources listed in the back of this book.

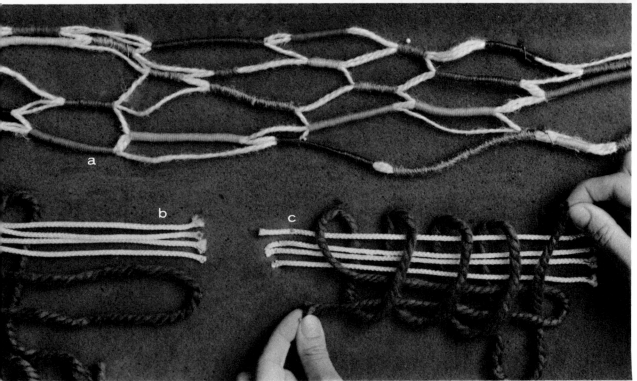

PERUVIAN WRAPPING.

Peruvian wrapping does not require a needle. It is especially convenient for wrapping a new cord over a group of cords and for thick cords that will not fit through the eye of a needle. (a) Example of finished wrapping with various color cords. (b) Lay out strands to be wrapped. Place the left end of cord that is to be used for the wrapping in a U-shape horizontal to the strands to be wrapped. Bring the right end of the wrapping cord over, around, and under the strands *and* under the U-shape as shown. (c) Continue to wind the wrapping cord until you are near the bottom of the U; on the last wind bring the right end of the cord through the U and hold it with your finger. Pull up the left end of the cord; release your finger; the right end will travel up with the pull to tighten the wrap. Cut the ends of the cord close to the wrap and tuck them under if necessary.

When wrapping, mix smooth and rough fibers and feel free to wrap them in various sizes, shapes, and colors. Found objects also may be strung or wrapped into the work as it progresses. In wrapping it is important to secure the ends of the fibers well beneath the wrapped layers by threading them in with a large-eye steel or plastic needle and dabbing them with white glue or fabric glue, if necessary.

Wrapping concepts are easy to visualize, and the methods are so simple that wrapping offers a marvelous opportunity to teach students of every age about fibers.

WRAPPING

OVERHAND KNOT WRAPPING.
The overhand knot is made by simply twisting one cord around another and pulling each end until the knot is tight. To wrap with the overhand knot make one knot at the front of the bundled cords and one knot at the back for as long as you wish the wrapping to be. Then thread the loose ends of the cord through a needle and pull them back up under the coil and secure them.

The wrap may be made with a single cord, or the cord may be doubled for greater thickness and faster progress. For variety you can wrap the knots close together or far apart.

WRAPPED HANGING.
Esther Robinson. Synthetic yarn, mercerized cotton, and dyed beads. Wrapping at different levels and in varying sizes creates a subtle rhythm.

14

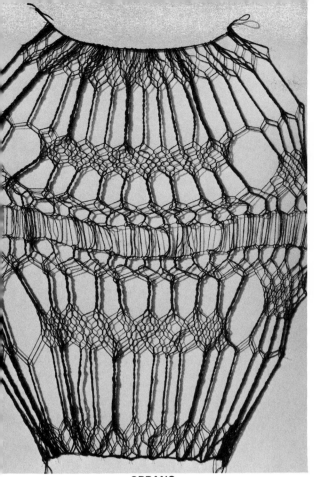

SPRANG.

Jeff Berman. A loose, open design achieved with sprang technique and thin cord.

STRUCTURED HANGING.
Dona Meilach. Sisal and jute. Length, 5½ feet. Twelve lengths of natural ½-inch sisal are doubled and wrapped with brown jute with the overhand knot wrap. Two sections of square knotting provide the bulging form. A sennit of half-knots *(see Chapter 3)* adds textural interest, which is repeated in the suspending cord.

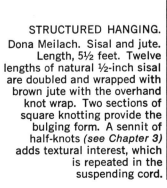

WRAPPING

MACRAMÉ FORM WITH WRAPPING.
Roger Thomason. Goat hair yarn, mohair, and camel hair yarn with duck feathers and cowrie shells. 24 inches high, 5 inches wide.
COLLECTION: PHOEBE MOONEY, KANSAS CITY

MACRAMÉ FORM WITH WRAPPING (Top detail). Roger Thomason. The wood ring that forms the hanger for this work is covered with knotted cord; then the wrapped cords are made to snake around the central knotted cylinder. Wrapping may be done close together or far apart. To achieve the horizontal striped effect in this piece, Mr. Thomason wraps with two different cords at one time arranging them carefully so that the colors alternate.

(Central detail). Cowrie shells are strung through drilled holes with doubled cord, which is placed horizontal to the main cords. Wrapping is used to encompass all cords. Observe how the base cords are allowed to emerge in different lengths for variety in color, spacing, and texture.

WRAPPING

CEREMONIAL WHIP.
Roger Thomason. Spanish yarn, goat hair, mohair, camel hair yarn, hawk feathers, and cowrie shells. 40 inches long.

(Detail of above). Wrapping in varying tones of natural colors with thick and thin cords. The handle core is a piece of wood.

18

CHIEFTAIN.
(Center detail of fabric sculpture). Jeanne Boardman
Knorr. Padded wool and velveteen with feathers
and wrapped wool yarn.
PHOTO: THOMAS BOOTH

BOAT.
Claudia Chapline. Metal assemblage with
yarn wrapped, glued, and sewn over form.
13 inches high, 19 inches wide.
PHOTO: LYN SMITH

MARDI GRAS.
Claudia Chapline. Hanging
structure of wrapped and
sewn yarn.
COURTESY: ARTIST

AUTUMN.
Claudia Chapline. Hanging
sculpture of wrapped and
tied yarn over wood and
metal with feathers.
PHOTO: DELL

21

WRAPPING

WRAPPED HANGING.
James Hines. Natural and blue dyed
jute.

ROPE VARIABLE.
Claudia Chapline. 50 feet of ½-inch
rope wrapped with wool yarn.
COURTESY: ARTIST

NECKPIECE WITH HAND-PAINTED BEADS.
(Opposite page, top left). Stana Coleman.

CHOKER.
(Opposite page, top right). Edie Mangun.
White linen.
PHOTO: GARLAND OWENS

NECKWEAR.
(Opposite page, bottom). Stana Coleman. Wrapped
jewelry ring holds the piece around the neck.
Wires were wrapped and wound around the ring.
The wires were bent and shaped, and pearl button
drops were added.

WRAPPING

OCTOPUS.
Evelyn Svec Ward. Sisal cords wrapped.
93 inches high, 10 inches wide.
COURTESY: ARTIST

BELL HANGING.
Evelyn Svec Ward. Wrapping with
sisals, wools, Mexican basket rings,
and bells. 10 feet long.
COURTESY: ARTIST

MOREL.
Evelyn Svec Ward. Fiber sculpture using wrapping and
stitching. Burlap was worked with cotton threads; then
rope and sisal wrapping were added. 14 inches high.
COURTESY: ARTIST

OCTOPOD.
Evelyn Svec Ward. Fiber
sculpture using same methods
as in *Morel*.
COURTESY: ARTIST

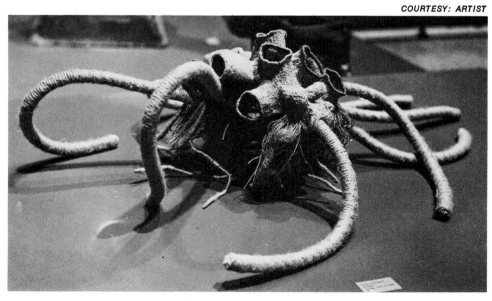

PERSONAGE.
Aurelia Muñoz. Sisal.
Macramé, predominantly in
vertical and horizontal
clove hitching.
COURTESY: ARTIST

knotting
macrame' and other methods

Craftsmen who are challenged by innovative techniques for forms that can be developed with familiar materials have added many kinds of knotting techniques to their accomplishments. Macrame' is one knotting art that involves tying two basic knots in infinite arrangements. Once popular with sailors for making such utilitarian items as bell covers, wheel covers, and other shipboard items, macrame' is now used to make hangings, sculpture, and unusual wearing apparel. The two easy-to-learn knots are the clove hitch and square knot.

Other knots not traditionally associated with macrame' also are legitimate additions to the knotter's repertoire and provide greater variety and interest than can be achieved with just the clove hitch and square knot. These additional knots may be found in contemporary macrame' publications and in knotting encyclopedias.

Part of the popularity of macrame' is due to its adaptability to other textile techniques; wrapping and macrame' are natural

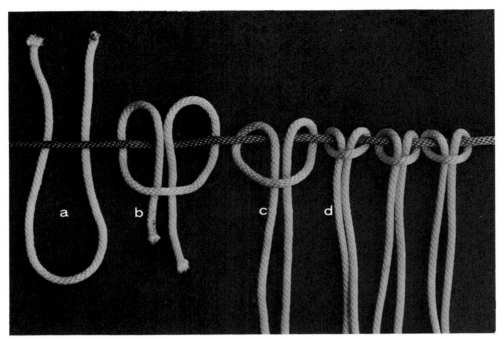

LARK'S HEAD MOUNTING.
Lark's head mounting is a method of attaching cords to a holding line so that they may be worked efficiently. (a) Double the cord and place it under the holding line. (b) Bring the two ends of the cord over the line and under the loop. (c) Pull and tighten the cord. (d) You will require a series of cords for knotting; usually the number should be divisible by four because square knotting utilizes four-cord multiples.

combinations. Macramé is also an adjunct to weaving, stitchery, knitting, crochet, and any art in which it will fit. Examples of macramé that have been combined with other techniques are illustrated here. These imaginative works underscore the modern approach to textile arts: there is no one pure use of any technique or material for its own sake. Anything goes together as long as it works in the mind and eye of the creator, and the artist fulfills his intention.

Knotting methods that were traditionally used in weaving by various primitive tribes also are being adapted and interestingly updated by increasing numbers of modern artists. Edie Mangun favors a Maori knot that is worked from two nails attached to a board, Ruben Steinberg employs a large curved needle to knot thick ropes. In this way he is able to achieve dizzying displays worked in burlap, leather, and other found materials that lend themselves to the composition and textural presentation.

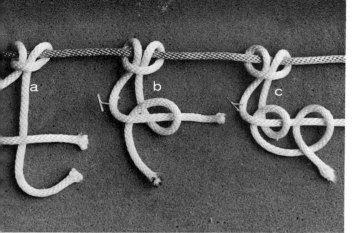

HORIZONTAL CLOVE HITCHING.

The clove hitch, tied horizontally, diagonally and vertically, is one of the basic macramé knots. Each cord is tied individually over an anchor cord. The angle of the anchor cord determines the angle of the finished bar of clove hitches. Left to right: (a) Pin the left hand cord to your board. Bring it horizontally *over* all the vertical cords. (b) With the next cord make a loop over, around, and under the anchor cord. (c) Make a second loop over, to the right of the knot, to the back and under the anchor cord. This completes the clove hitch.

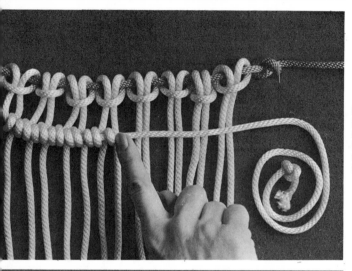

Continue tying each cord individually over the same anchor cord, pushing each knot close to the anchor cord. If you do not pin or hold the anchor cord tight across the knotting cords, the knots will not form properly. If you tend to forget which cord is the anchor, identify it by tying a knot on the end.

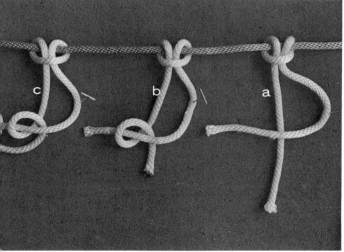

To carry the knotting back again: (a) pin the anchor cord at the right side and reverse the knot procedure; (b) make the first loop over around and behind the anchor cord; (c) make the second loop to the left of the first, over, around, and under the anchor.

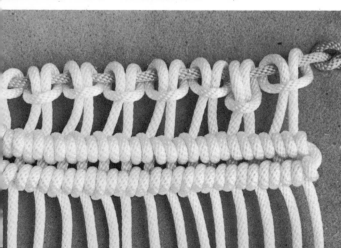

TWO COMPLETED CLOVE HITCH BARS. In clove hitch patterns an anchor used back and forth will be used up more quickly than the knotting cords. With experience you will learn to make anchor cords longer than knotting cords. Remember, new anchor cords may be picked up anywhere in the work to create short, long, and angled clove hitch bars, as illustrated in examples that follow.

29

KNOTTING DIAGONAL CLOVE HITCHING. Most macramé designs are made by changing the direction of the clove hitch bars. This is done by holding the anchor cord in the direction you wish the bar to take and continuing to clove hitch. Anchor cords do *not* always have to be end cords. A cord may be picked up anywhere in the knotting and used as an anchor cord for angled, short, and long clove hitch bars.

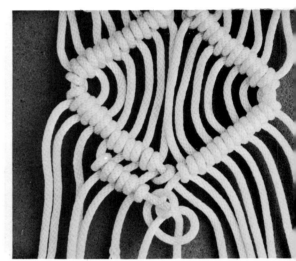

To make the top legs of an X, use an end cord from each side, pin them over the knotting cords, and join them in the center of the work. Clove hitch the cords on the left side from left to right and those on the right side from right to left. Continue the X shape by pinning the anchor cords back out to the ends as in the bottom half of the X and continue clove hitching.

For a diamond pattern pick up the two center cords for anchors. Pin them out to place over the knotting cords and pin to each side. Clove hitch the cords on the left side from the center out; do the same on the right side. For the bottom half of the diamond bring the anchors back toward the center (as in the photo above) and continue to clove hitch to complete the pattern. The extra bar at the bottom illustrates how easily you can pick up any cord in the work to create a half bar.

To make a circular form, pin a holding line to your board and lark's head your knotting cords around the circle. Continue to use the central circle cord as the anchor cord for additional clove hitching. New circular anchor cords can be added anywhere in the work by pinning them over the knotting cords and continuing the knotting. Cords for a circular work may also be mounted on a hard plastic or metal ring.

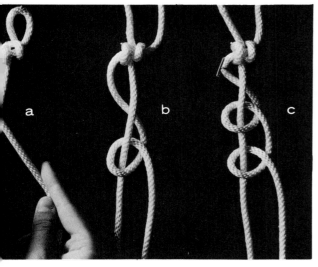

VERTICAL CLOVE HITCHING. Many of the knotted art forms use the vertical clove hitch. This knot differs from bar clove hitching in that each knotting cord changes its role and becomes an anchor cord for a continuous knotting cord. For vertical hitches one long cord is used for knotting, and each previous knotting cord becomes the anchor for the long cord. Because one cord is used for vertical hitching, it is used up very quickly. You must allow extra cord or add cord when you plan to use this knot.

VERTICAL CLOVE HITCH LEFT TO RIGHT.

(a) Place a pin to the left side of the work to hold the knotting cord. Bring the knotting cord (previously an anchor cord) *under* the first vertical strand on the left.

(b) Loop the knotting cord over the new vertical anchor to the front, then around and through for the first half of the knot.

(c) The second half of the knot is looped over the vertical cord and around it as illustrated.

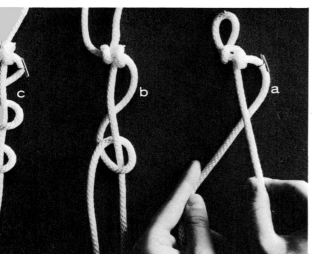

VERTICAL CLOVE HITCH RIGHT TO LEFT.

The procedure is exactly the opposite of the vertical clove hitch left to right.

(a) Pin the knotting cord to the right side of the work and bring the knotting cord *under* the first verticle strand on the right.

(b) Loop the knotting cord to the right over the vertical strand, around and through at the top of the loop.

(c) Make the second half of the hitch over the anchor to the right, around the top of the loop and through. Continue by bringing the knotting cord under each strand and repeating the directions of the loops for the knot until the row is completed.

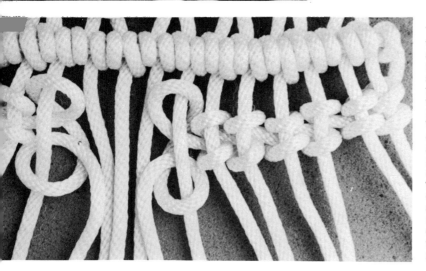

The vertical clove hitch from left to right is shown on the left side, and the vertical clove hitch from right to left is shown on the right side. When the row is completed, the knots will be pushed up together. In a thinner cord they lie closer together and tighter. Vertical clove hitches may be made over more than one anchor cord at a time. The vertical clove hitch provides a good place to introduce a second color cord because vertical hitching requires extra long cords, for which you may not have allowed in the original measurement. The ends can be camouflaged in the back of the work by weaving in, stitching, or gluing later.

#37.

Rosita Montgomery. Metal hoop, shades of gold wool rug yarn, and black horsehair. 40 inches in diameter. All horizontal and vertical clove hitches are used in this composition, which begins from a central ring and expands. New knotting cords in different shades are easily added by doubling them and clove hitching over anchor cords. Cords that become too short may be dropped at the back; new cords can be added, and the knotting can be continued. Added cords may be tied at the back of the piece, or worked in with a crochet hook. Loose ends can be secured into the piece with any white emulsion glue.

PHOTO: LEE PAYNE

Macramé is accomplished by mounting multiples of cords on a holding line such as a dowel, another cord, or an object, using a lark's head knot; then the basic knots are tied. The beginner should practice tying the knots by pinning the cords to a knotting board such as a cushion, a square of polyfoam, or anything that will hold pins. After you have become adept at tying the knots, you can work from a rod mounted on a hook, from a hoop attached to a door frame, or from whatever base is convenient for a particular project.

Cords for macramé are available from hardware stores and cord suppliers listed in the back of the book. Cords that can be used include synthetic yarns, ropes such as linen, jute, sisal, and manila, cotton and nylon seine twine, rayon cord, braided and twisted polypropylene, and any string or rope that can hold a knot. Cords may readily be dyed either before or after the knotting has been completed.

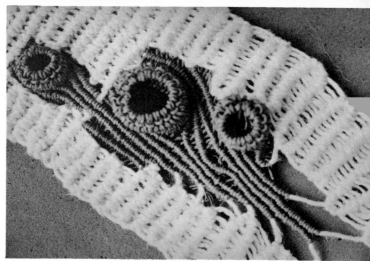

STUDY IN BROWN AND BEIGE.
Susan Meilach. Clove hitching was worked over a cardboard tube to achieve a three-dimensional shape. After the tube was removed, the cord retained the shape. Ends were clove hitched into a flat beige background, which also was clove hitched.

BLACK MACRAMÉ WIG.
Lee Erlin Snow. Beginning from a circle pinned directly into the plastic foam wigstand at the top of the head, the work was expanded with multiple strands of cords for anchors to create thin and thick areas. Some wrapping also was used. Macramé designs may be symmetrical, as at the left, or worked in a free, abstract manner.
PHOTO: BOB LOPEZ

Cord lengths needed for macramé depend on cord thickness and knotting design. For close knotting patterns each knotting length from holding line to end usually should be four times the finished length desired. Therefore, when you use doubled cords on a holding line, cut them eight times the desired finished length. For large projects it often helps to knot a size gauge to determine the amount of cord needed so you won't have to piece it as you work.

Found objects, springs, sea shells, ceramic pieces, and stone-ware beads are all valuable adjuncts to macramé. In addition to the knots, wrapping (illustrated in Chapter 2) may be used for ending work, for covering fibers, or for free-standing pieces.

After you have learned to tie knots, you will find it relatively easy to understand what is happening in a finished macramé object by simply looking at a photo and studying the square knot and clove hitch arrangements.

KNOTTING THE SQUARE KNOT.

Mount sets of two folded cords (four strands) for each square knot. The two center cords become the anchors, and the two outside cords are used for knotting. Square knotting patterns usually require sets of four strands and, therefore, are easiest to do when multiples of four knotting strands are mounted.

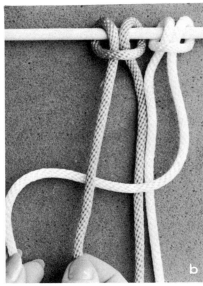

(a) Place right cord over and to the left of the two anchor cords.

(b) Place the left cord over the right cord.

(c) Bring the left cord under the right cord, under anchors, and through the loop formed by the right cord.

(d) Pull both cords. You now have the first half of the square knot.

(e) Place the left cord over the two anchors.

(f) Place the right cord over the left cord.

(g) Bring the right cord under the left cord, under the two anchors, and through the loop formed by the left cord.

(h) Pull both cords. You now have the finished square knot.

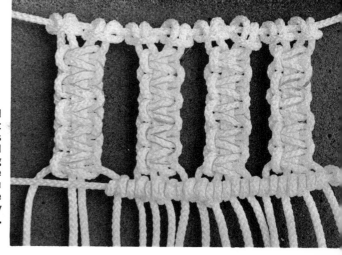

Rows of square knot sennits (lengths of knotted cords) will look like this. As you become proficient at square knotting, you can change the multiples of cords used in a square knot for variations and cross over rows for additional square knotting motifs. As you study the examples, you will see many ways of using the square knot. Once you have learned to tie the knot, you will have little trouble understanding what is happening in any examples.

An alternating square knot pattern is the foundation of many macramé designs.
  (a) Tie a row of square knots across all the work using a multiple of four cords.
  (b) For the second row drop the first two cords; square knot with the next four. Knot each next group of four cords until the row is completed with two cords remaining at end.
  (c) Tie the third row the same as the first. Continue the pattern, dropping the first two cords in every other row.

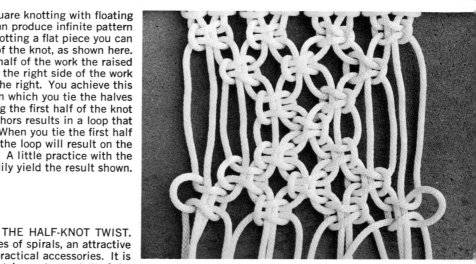

The progression of square knotting with floating (unknotted cords) can produce infinite pattern variations. When knotting a flat piece you can balance the raised loop of the knot, as shown here. Observe that in the left half of the work the raised loop is on the left; on the right side of the work the raised loop is on the right. You achieve this by reversing the order in which you tie the halves of the square knot. Tying the first half of the knot to the left of the anchors results in a loop that appears on the left side. When you tie the first half of the knot to the right, the loop will result on the right side of the knot. A little practice with the square knot will readily yield the result shown.

THE HALF-KNOT TWIST.
This twist results in a series of spirals, an attractive detail for art work and practical accessories. It is made very easily by tying *only one half* of the square knot continuously. To make the spiral twist to the left tie only the *first half of the knot:* the *right* cord over the anchors to the *left* for about seven ties per twist, depending upon the thickness of the cord used. To make the cords twist to the right use the *second half only* of the square knot, tying all the knots with the *left* cord over the anchors to the *right,* as shown. The tighter you pull the knotted cords, the more they will twist.

MOUNTAIN MOSS.
Clara Creager. Cowhair yarn
in shades of greens and dark
browns and mounted on a
hayrake tooth. Square knots and
horizontal and vertical clove
hitches.
PHOTO: RICHARD ZIMMER

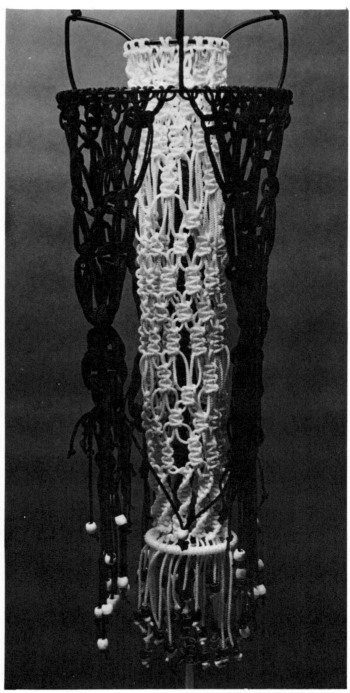

GOLD MACRAMÉ CASCADE.
Virginia Haas. Yarn with thin brass metal cut into circles, strung on work, and wrapped on ends. A sennit of half-knot twists was used to create the bow.

BLACK AND WHITE CYLINDER.
Dona Meilach. Black and white Macra-Cord mounted on a wrought iron frame. The white cylinder is held out at the bottom by clove hitching over a plastic circle from a bracelet. Each panel of black utilizes square knotting in a different way. A black and white twist sennit is dropped through the center of the work.

KNOTTING

COME'TE DANS UN ESPACE ENCLOS.
Aurelia Muñoz. Linen and
nylon cord is a plastic box.
COURTESY: ARTIST

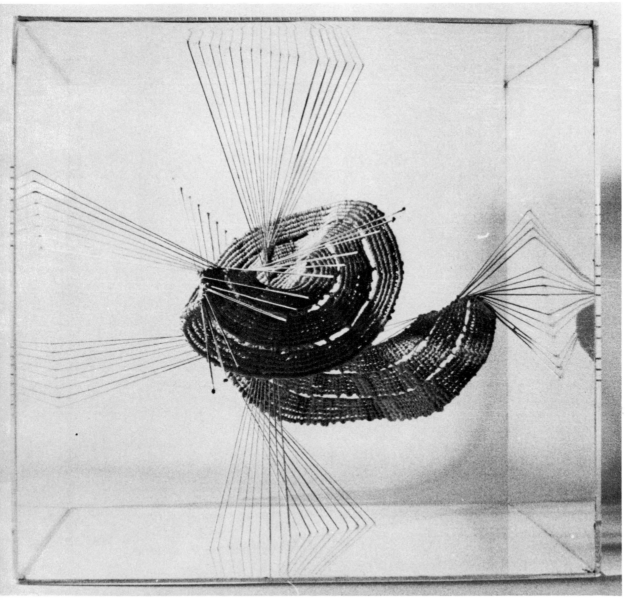

MACRAMÉ ON A STIRRUP.
Joyce Barnes. Front and
back. Jute, horsehair, leather,
hawk feathers, and beads.

SEA SHAPES.
Lorraine Ohlson. White
cotton twine and jute
mounted on black felt and
framed.

PIZZA PIE IN THE SKY.
Lee Erlin Snow. Mixed yarns worked in
macramé and free crochet and mounted
on a hula hoop. 4 feet, 6 inches high.

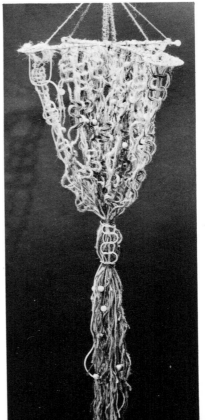

INTERNAL REARRANGEMENT #7.
Dona Meilach. Natural and brown jute
with rawhide mounted on two rattan
paddles crossed over to create a structure
different from the usual cylindrical or flat
macramé form. 5 feet high.

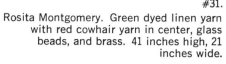

#31.
Rosita Montgomery. Green dyed linen yarn with red cowhair yarn in center, glass beads, and brass. 41 inches high, 21 inches wide.
PHOTO: LEE PAYNE

SMALL CASCADE.
Berni Gorski. ⅛-inch cotton traverse cord on a 13-inch diameter plastic circle. 23 inches long.

PHOTO: HERNY GORSKI

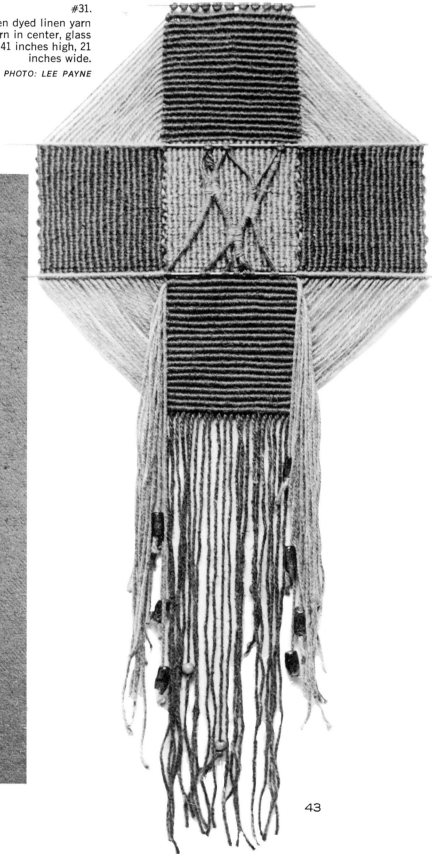

43

DRIFTWOOD WITH MACRAMÉ.
Lee Erlin Snow. This convertible
piece may be hung on a wall or tacked
to the front of a simple dress.
PHOTO: BOB LOPEZ

CEREMONY.
Nancy J. Koehler. Natural jute.
Full-length macramé dress with metal
rings incorporated into the knotting.
COURTESY: ARTIST

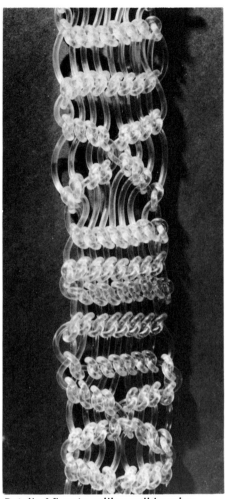

Detail of floor to ceiling wall hanging of polyvinyl chloride cords. Rhonda Ronan. This piece shows one of the many materials that may be used for macramé.

PHOTO: COURTESY, ARTIST

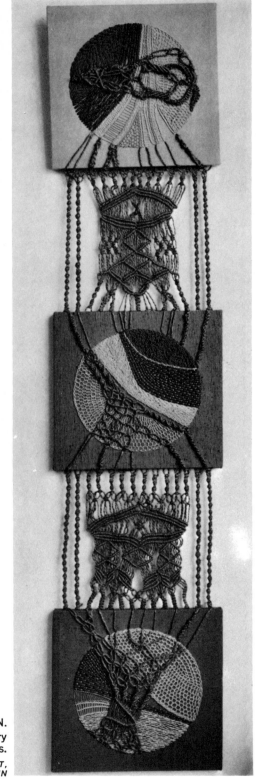

COMPOSITION.
Virginia Tiffany. Macramé with stitchery over fabric-covered wood frames.

PHOTOGRAPHED AT ART INDEPENDENT, LAKE GENEVA, WISCONSIN

Edie Mangun has explored the knotting techniques of primitive cultures and has developed a modern interpretation of Maori tribe knot techniques. In many of her pieces the fibers are worked with the Maori knot, macramé knots, wrapping, and finger weaving. She uses a board and simple twining techniques, shown on the following pages.

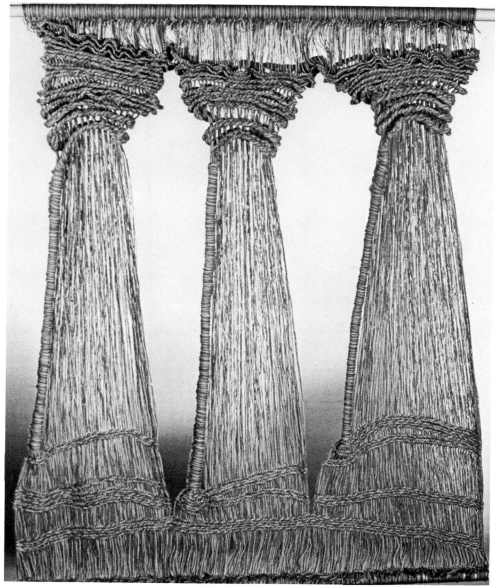

WALL HANGING.
Edie Mangun. Purple wool.
Maori knot with wrapping.

ORANGE NODUS STUDY
(opposite page, left).
Edie Mangun. Nodus, which means a knotty situation, was developed very simply over the knotting board that the artist developed.

ALL PHOTOS: COURTESY, ARTIST

TONES OF GREEN NODUS STUDY
(opposite page, right).
Edie Mangun.

47

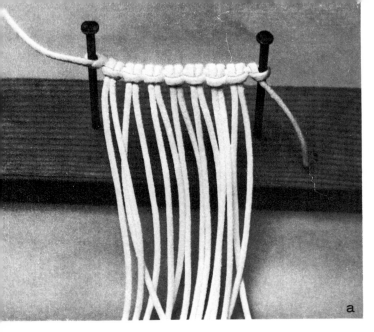

(a) The Maori knot is worked from two nails hammered into a board at the distance desired for the width of the finished piece. Tie one horizontal cord between the nails, making sure that it is taut. Mount vertical cords to fill the horizontal cord, using the clove hitch as in macramé.

(b) The principle is to work with groups of four cords and to weave them as follows: take the first cord and weave it under, over, and under the next three cords; pull the loose end of the cord up to the top of the work as shown.

(c) Pick up the second cord and weave it over, under, and over the next three cords, again bringing the loose end *tight* up to the top of the work. Continue to weave each successive cord until you have decreased to one remaining cord.

(d) When the row of cords has been woven and each end is pulled up, your work will look like this. To make the turn for the next row, pull the final cord around the nail to the other side of the work.

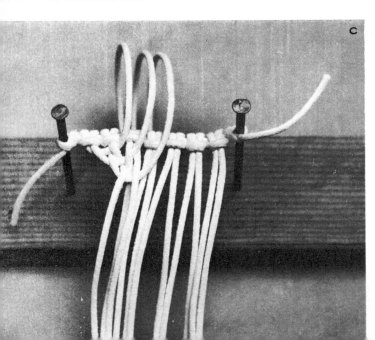

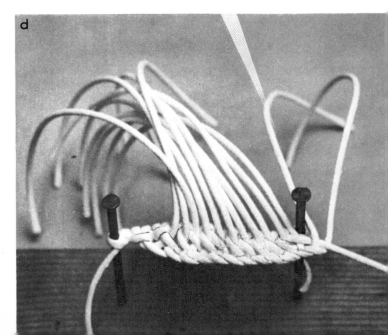

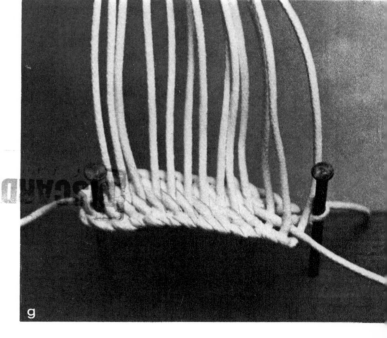

(e) Turn the piece around, wood and all, so that the ends that have been knotted up are now heading down. Repeat the same weaving process with the four-cord multiples as the one in the first row.

(f) As you knot, it is important to pull the knotted ends close to the top of the work.

(g) At the end of the second row, again bring the final cord around the nail; then turn the work around and repeat the procedure.

(h) Two completed rows in heavy cord will have a very obvious knot pattern. A finished end may be removed from the nail. Maori knot rows can be combined with macramé knots, and colored cord may be used to create interesting effects. The appearance of the Maori knot differs greatly, depending upon the size and texture of the cord used.

PHOTO SERIES:
COURTESY, EDIE MANGUN

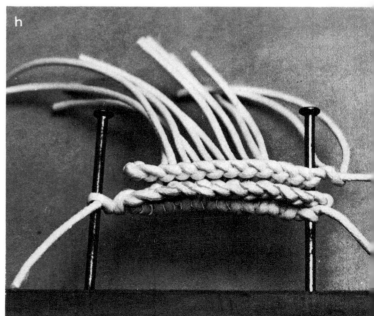

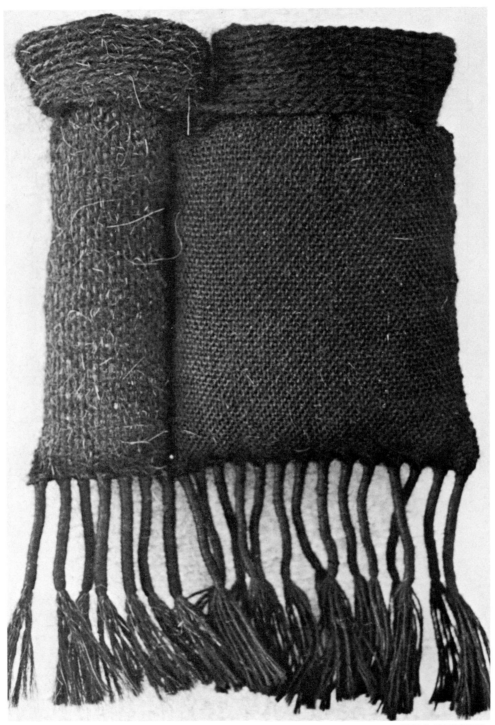

WALL HANGING.
Edie Mangun. Three-dimensional hanging of mohair and
horsehair composed of the Maori knot and wrapping.
18 inches high, 12 inches wide.
PHOTO: COURTESY, ARTIST

SPRING BOUQUET.
Edie Mangun. The Maori knot worked around the nails and pulled to shape results in three-dimensional forms that may be grouped and combined with wrapping. 6 inches by 6 inches.
PHOTO: COURTESY, ARTIST

51

TOTEM.
Ruben Steinberg.

RUBEN STEINBERG'S KNOTTED ROPE STRUCTURES.

Ruben Steinberg has created a unique art form using fibers and some fabrics to achieve virile, highly textured, and unusual surfaces and shapes. He thinks of this art form as an extension of a collage theory devised by Picasso, who used rope around a picture to take the place of a frame. Mr. Steinberg adapts heavy rope and cord that usually have been discarded. Some rolls of cord that he has used were in a fire and were badly water-soaked. Much of the thinner cord was taken from draperies and shades that were destined for the garbage heap.

Basically Mr. Steinberg uses a repitition of the clove hitch. Because the ropes are so heavy, he uses a pair of needle-nose pliers to handle the cords in order to avoid wear and tear on his fingers. The knotted ropes become so stiff that they often are used to form a relief dimension.

BANNER.
Ruben Steinberg.

STUDY FOR A
DOORMAT.
Ruben Steinberg.

53

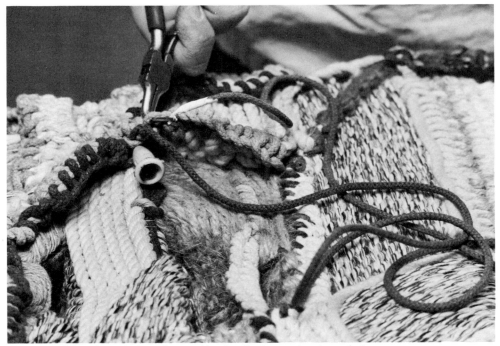

Ruben Steinberg's technique for creating knotted rope structures is to repeat the knots. But the knots are threaded through a previous row of knots rather than tied over a holding cord. He uses thick cords and wraps the end with masking tape to facilitate pulling it through the loop of a knot in the previous row with a needle-nose pliers.

He holds the first loop . . .

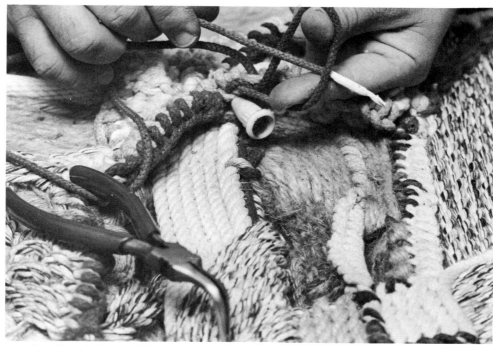

. . . then threads the cord through the loop and . . .

. . . pulls it tight to create row on row of the knots. The types of knots are unimportant as long as the intended result is achieved.

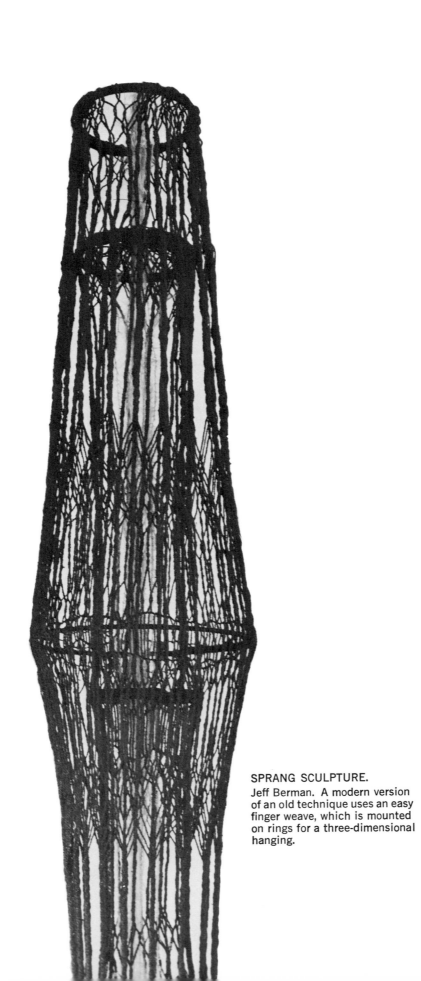

SPRANG SCULPTURE.
Jeff Berman. A modern version
of an old technique uses an easy
finger weave, which is mounted
on rings for a three-dimensional
hanging.

sprang
or meshwork

Sprang, like macramé, may be a new word in your vocabulary. And like macramé, sprang is an ancient technique that is enjoying a revival as the textile arts continue to grow. Through the centuries sprang has been called Egyptian plaitwork, meshwork, knotless netting, and frame braiding, among other names. Sprang resembles netting, but the fibers are not knotted; rather, they are twisted around one another. Historically sprang has been created by using sticks and bobbins and usually has been worked on a frame.

The distinctive twist of the sprang system has been found in textile examples from ancient Peru. Paintings on early Greek vases show women making open meshwork with fibers. Today you can find sprang hammocks and shopping bags made in Mexico. Some work is also found in Scandinavia. However, as craftsmen begin to use sprang, you will see this technique exhibited as framed lacelike structures and three-dimensional sculptures.

SPRANG (a) Materials for sprang are a nonstretch cord, two wood dowels for each end, short dowels or straws to insert through the twists to hold them *(see photo i)*, masking tape, needle, scissors, and two C clamps to create tension. Hoops and wire are used to make the piece three dimensional.

WARPING THE CORD.

(b) Warping may be accomplished over the legs of an upturned chair or any two uprights; but do be sure that you can remove the cords without loosening them. Tie the figure 8.

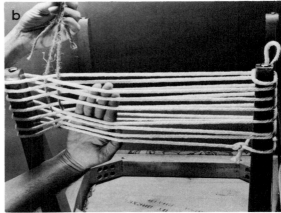

Craftsman Jeff Berman has developed a simple method of creating sprang that requires only cord or string, a table top, two C clamps, masking tape, dowels, and straws, sticks, or knitting needles to act as a temporary weft between each row as it is twisted.

Sprang actually consists of warped cords twisted around each other; no weft cords are used, as they are in weaving. The number of photos in the accompanying demonstration makes sprang appear complicated, but it is really so amazingly simple and fun to do that once you have followed the sequence you can easily make extremely complex structures—your fingers will twist the cords almost automatically.

Consider the demonstration in three steps: (1) warping, or winding, on the cords, (2) interweaving the cords for the pattern, and (3) locking the center. The result will be a flat, stretchy

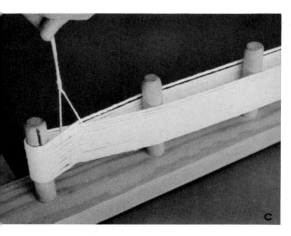

(c) Warping (or winding) the cords correctly is part of the secret for doing sprang successfully. Use two uprights of a warping board or any two uprights set a desired distance apart (the posts of two chairs or the legs of a chair for examples). Warping must be fairly tight, so be sure you can slip the cords over the end easily (do not use drawer handles or knobs that are wider at the top than at the bottom). Tie the first end around one upright; then wind the cord so that you have a figure 8 in the resulting winds. The number of cords warped on will determine the density of the piece. For a sampler begin with at least 16 warps. Tie the loose end at the same pole as the beginning end; push the figure 8 to the opposite end and tie a string loosely around the figure 8, as shown, to result in 2 layers of cords. Count your cords. Be sure that you have the same number of cords on the top and bottom layers.

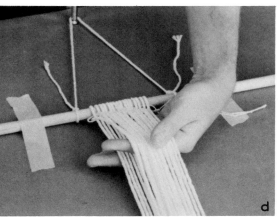

(d) Place a dowel rod at each end of the looped cords. At the top end place the dowel above the figure 8; at the bottom end be sure to place dowels in the loops of the loose cords. Keep the cords orderly. Place one C clamp at each end of a table and tape the dowel rods as far apart as possible so that the cords are tight. Then tie a piece of cord to the dowel and around the bottom of the C clamp, as shown (see photo i). As the work begins to tighten, you may have to release the tension of one end. With the tension properly set lift the top layer of cords from the bottom layer, push the figure 8 tie to the top (do not untie it until you have finished the piece, and begin weaving).

meshwork that can be pulled to a shape and mounted. It may be formed around hoops that are tied or woven into the work; then the sprang may be joined to form a sculpture.

Sprang itself is so elastic that a hard-finish, fairly strong cord with little stretch and little nap is best. In the accompanying demonstration cable cord was used; but polished cotton twine, seine twine, clothesline, jute, and other nonstretch fibers are excellent. When it is stretched, the finished piece will lose about 25 percent of its length, so if a finished specific length is required, warp on cords long enough to allow for stretch loss.

Sprang can be combined with macramé and weaving, stiffened with casting resin (see page 83), used for collage, and worked in any other manner you like.

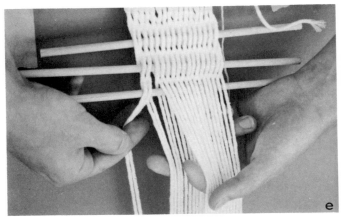

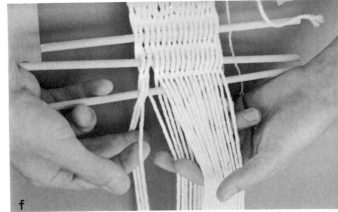

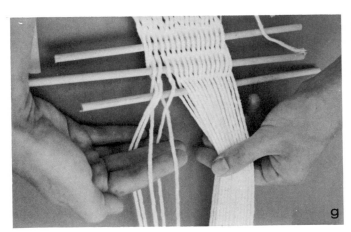

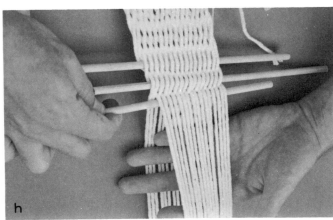

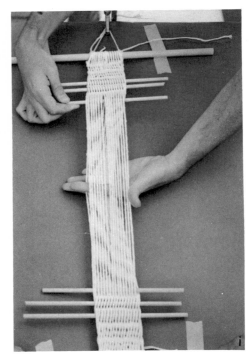

INTERWEAVING.

(e) The weaving system consists basically of two rows that interlock as a horizontal, or "weft," stick is placed between them. Here the weave is shown as it is done on the third row, but you begin the first row and all odd-numbered rows the same way. Keep the two layers of cords separated with one hand. With the other hand take the first two upper warps and drop them down to the left.

(f) Pick up the first *single* bottom warp, lift, and hold.

(g) Take the next single top warp and drop it to the left; then pick up, lift, and hold the next single bottom warp. Continue a one-cord drop and one-cord pick-up all across the row, bringing up the last two bottom yarns. (Note: you must end with the same number of yarns you picked up at the beginning of the row. For example, if you dropped two to begin, you must end with two.)

(h) Place a stick between the two layers and . . .

(i) . . . run your hand down to the bottom. The same weave will result. Place a stick between these two layers also.
 For the second row and all even-numbered rows you must lock the stitch by alternating the weave. Pick up *only the first cord from the warp* and, as in odd-numbered rows, continue with a one-cord drop and one-cord pick up across the row. Always place a dowel at the top and bottom ends. As the rows progress and each row is locked, you can pull out the first sticks and use them again.
 For the third row repeat the first, taking the first two upper warps, then one lower. Continuing a one-cord drop and one-cord pick-up, ending with two cords.

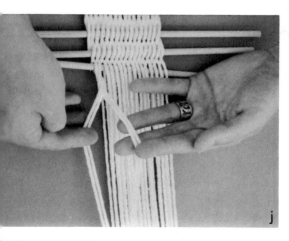

DECORATIVE "LEGS."

(j) After you have mastered the two simple rows, you can begin to experiment with different weaving progressions to create decorative "legs." For an open, more lacy pattern, Jeff Berman picks up two cords from the top and two from the bottom and twists them around each other. *(see photo o).*

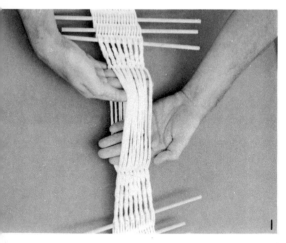

(k) Continue twisting two upper and two lower cords around each other. End with upper warps in the upper position.

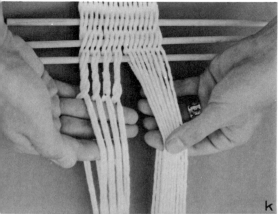

(l) Push hard against the twist at both the top and the bottom.

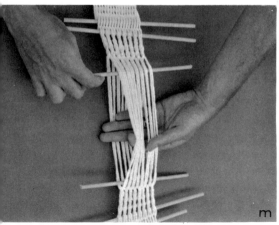

(m) Use dowels to hold them secure. Decorative legs must be locked in place with another two-row sequence of the basic weave.

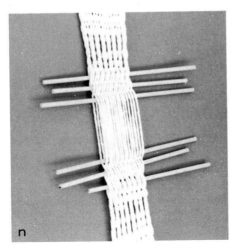

(n) You can change the weave in any row to create both decorative legs and the basic weave. If you change the number of cords used for the basic weave, another variation occurs, but the ratio must follow a 2-1 and 1-1 sequence (first row, 4-2; second row, 2-2, etc.)

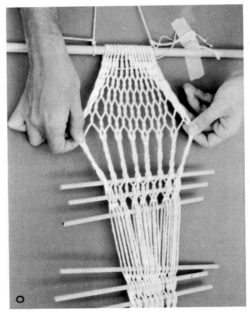

(o) When the sprang is stretched, the basic two rows and the decorative legs can be easily recognized. Below the legs two additional basic rows lock the legs in place. In a closed weaving system, whatever happens at the top happens at the bottom. However, you can create a different effect by allowing more space between the dowels.

LOCKING THE CENTER.
This method of locking the center allows tremendous stretch. If the cords are too tight to continue weaving, loosen the tension at one end of the C clamp and/or remove all but the last two sets of dowels, top and bottom. Keep the dowels straight.

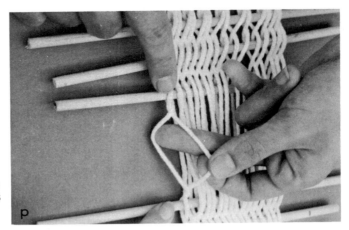

(p) Take the first upper and first lower warp; twist them around each other so that the upper one is on top. Push the twisted yarns as tight as possible against the dowels on each end.

(q) Take the next lower warp and pull it up through the loop on your fingers. Push the ends against the dowels.

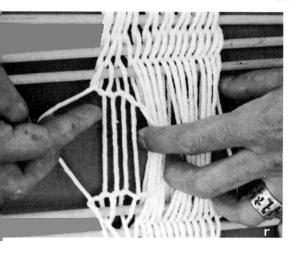

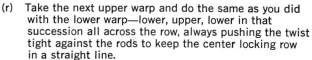

(r) Take the next upper warp and do the same as you did with the lower warp—lower, upper, lower in that succession all across the row, always pushing the twist tight against the rods to keep the center locking row in a straight line.

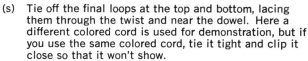

(s) Tie off the final loops at the top and bottom, lacing them through the twist and near the dowel. Here a different colored cord is used for demonstration, but if you use the same colored cord, tie it tight and clip it close so that it won't show.

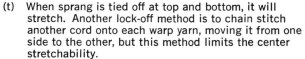

(t) When sprang is tied off at top and bottom, it will stretch. Another lock-off method is to chain stitch another cord onto each warp yarn, moving it from one side to the other, but this method limits the center stretchability.

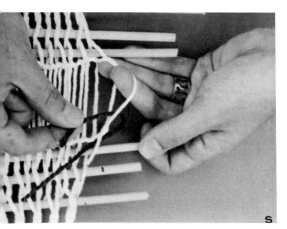

(u) Untie the original cord that held the figure 8. Lace a cord through the loops just below the dowels at top and bottom. *Never* allow the ends of the original dowel to become loose or the entire finished piece will unwind. When the cord is laced through, you can remove the dowels.

(v) Finished sprang can be shaped and mounted on a board. A short tie-off cord at the top and bottom will keep the ends closed. A longer cord will allow them to expand. The piece may be shaped over a series of rings or hoops, which can be secured by tying in. After you have finished a work of sprang, your imagination will be stimulated by the many shapes into which it can be stretched.

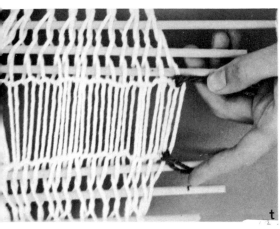

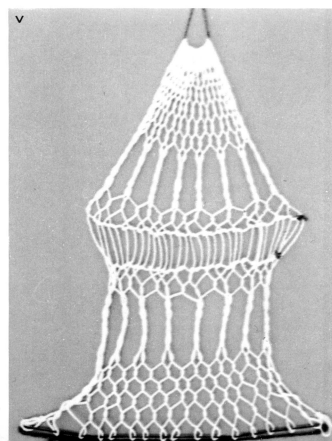

SCULPTURE.
Jeff Berman. Wrapped rings were tied into the finished sprang; then the bottom ring was lifted back up into the center and tied in. A group of knotted cords is added for a central core.

ASYMMETRY.
Sprang usually results in a symmetrical arrangement of cords, but this can be altered by the wires used and the arrangement of the movement of the piece.
STUDENT OF JEFF BERMAN

BODY ENVIRONMENT II.
Joy Wulke. A hanging body net made of cotton clothesline twine using sprang and macramé with stoneware beads.
COURTESY: ARTIST

65

CROCHETED HANGINGS.
Jane Knight. All pieces crocheted
with rug wool.
PHOTO: RICHARD KNIGHT

crochet and knitting

With crochet and knitting well established as needlework techniques, you might ask, "What can be created with them that hasn't already been done?" The answer can be found in the following pages. Artists familiar with these popular techniques are discovering fascinating ways in which they can work yarns to create impressive shapes.

Three-dimensional pieces used as hangings and body coverings are among the most startling uses of crochet. Some artists deftly combine knitting and crochet with netmaking, sprang, lacemaking, and other methods. Estelle Carlson uses a plastic casting resin to stiffen a sculpture and to impart a gravity defying appearance in her tubular weaving.

Many nontraditional crochet fibers are used today, including rug yarn, jute, and yak hair spun into strands. Some works shown here have been created as jewelry, but they have all the traditional

MAN.
Jeff Berman. Crocheted cord
and twine with wrapping.

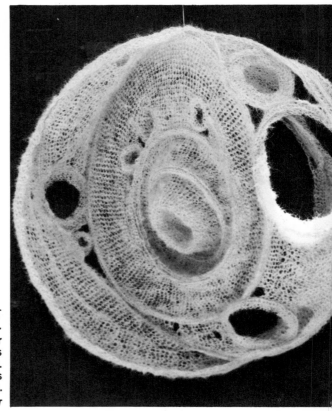

YAK HAIR CROCHET
HANGING.
Silvia Heyden. Yak hair
handspun by the artist is
worked over a wire frame.
46 inches by 46 inches
by 10 inches.
COURTESY: ARTIST

components of a work of art: shape, space, line, form, and texture
and are visually as well as texturally interesting.

Basic crochet and knitting stitches are generally used to create
these works, but the stitches may be worked over metal or plastic
rings to support the form. Specific stitches are not illustrated
because they are so numerous and are readily available in needlework books and magazines. The examples are offered to stimulate
ideas that you can tap to create your own designs and to familiarize
you with the variety of approaches already achieved; they are not
offered as patterns to be copied.

You might begin by learning the crochet chains and simply
working in a free crochet manner. If you are already adept with
a crochet hook and knitting needles, you can probably begin by
visualizing a form, then trying to work it out by using your own
ingenuity.

CROCHETED HANGINGS.
Jane Knight. All pieces crocheted
with rug wool. Lengths vary
from 4½ feet to 12 feet.

PHOTO: RICHARD KNIGHT

COME AND SIT ON GRANDMA'S KNEE.
Bonnie Meltzer. Bodies of life size figures are stuffed solidly for
support, but arms and legs are soft and pliable so that their positions
may be changed. The seat areas are flat for seating, and laps may be
sat upon. Many types of yarns and flat and looped stitches are used.
PHOTO: WES TAFT

70

I ALWAYS WANTED TO BE A BLONDE RATHER THAN
A RAVEN-HAIRED BEAUTY.
Bonnie Meltzer. Crocheted body coverings. Real people inside both
crocheted pieces. The figure at right becomes a moving sculptural form.
Fabric strips, rug yarn, and sheared sheepskin were combined with fabric.

PHOTO: WES TAFT

CROCHET
AND KNITTING

PORTRAIT OF AN OLD LOVER
AS A NEW MAN.
Bonnie Meltzer. Rayon crochet and needle
lace over a plexiglass form. 18 inches high,
10 inches wide at base.
PHOTO: WES TAFT

CHRIST FIGURE.
Jane Knight. Crochet over a wood base
with stuffed figure using rug yarn. 4½
feet high.
PHOTO: RICHARD KNIGHT

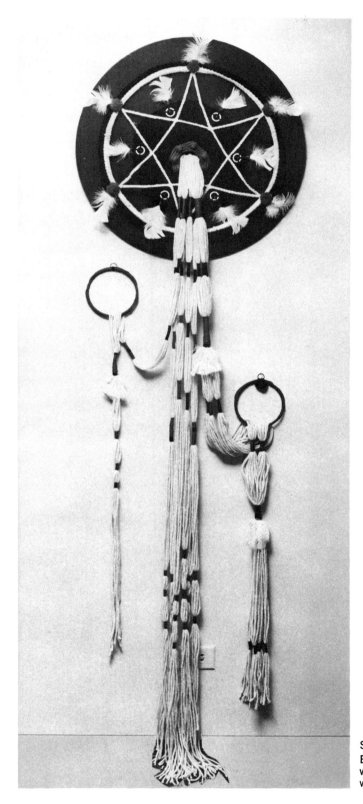

SHIELD.
Esther Robinson. Crochet
with fabric, feathers, and
wrapping. 5½ feet high.

73

YAK HAIR RELIEF.
Silvia Heyden. Organic forms are achieved with
the hand-spun yak hair, which has a silky, soft
feel with a fuzzy texture.

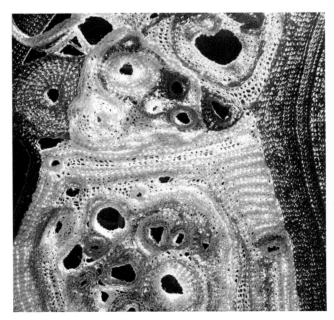

Detail of a space divider of
crocheted linen by Silvia
Heyden uses positive and
negative shapes with light
playing an important role in
the composition.

YAK HAIR HANGING.
Silvia Heyden. Three views. Crochet
over a bent wire frame results in a
sculptural form.
PHOTOS: COURTESY, ARTIST

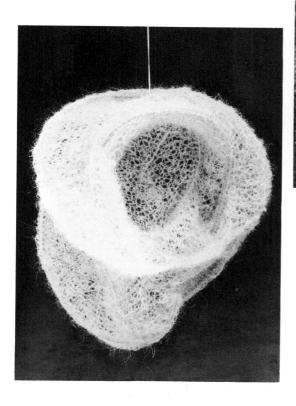

CROCHET
AND KNITTING

NECKPIECE *(top right).*
Norma Minkowitz. Crochet,
beading, and fringing.
COURTESY: ARTIST

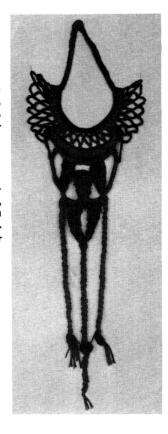

NECKPIECE *(top left).*
Norma Minkowitz. Crochet,
braiding, and fringing with
3-ply Persian wool yarn.
COURTESY: ARTIST

Body adornments offer stimulating ideas for crochet.

ARM ADORNMENT
Jeanne Boardman Knorr. Cotton cord with wood beads.

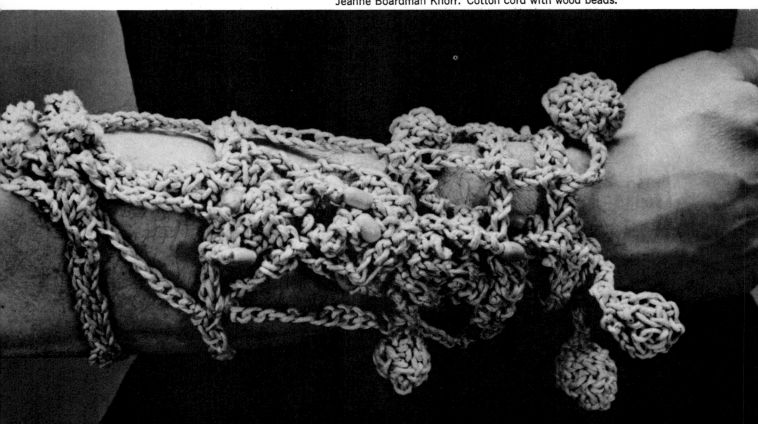

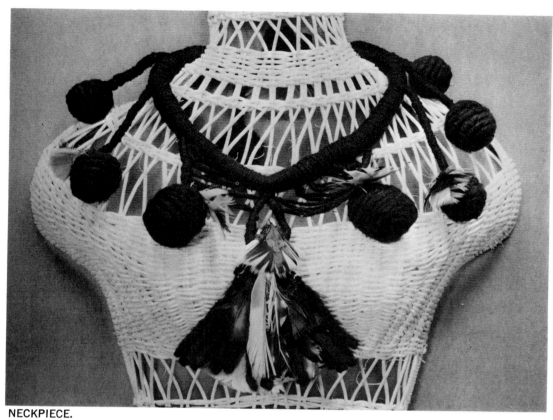

NECKPIECE.
Jeanne Boardman Knorr. Crochet, wrapping, and feathers.

NECK ADORNMENT WITH EAR ENVIRONMENTS.
Jeanne Boardman Knorr.

HEAD ADORNMENT.
Jeanne Boardman Knorr.
Cotton yarn.

KING AND QUEEN.
Esther Robinson. Knit wall panel mounted over a board. Some overstitching with running stitches. Beads incorporated.

CROCHETED LAYERED CIRCLE.
Pat Baldwin. Raffia, wool, and jute. 14 inches in diameter.
COURTESY: ARTIST

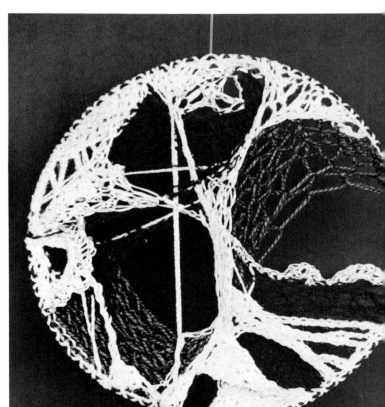

WINTER WEB.
Evelyn Svec Ward. Burlap, chenille, jute, synthetics, cotton, and linen in white, browns, naturals, and tans. Knitting and needlework. 38 inches high, 34 inches wide.

COLLECTION: MR. & MRS. ALAN B. KUPER, CLEVELAND, OHIO

CROCHET AND KNITTING

Estelle Carlson has developed an individual method of using a simple fiber technique, sometimes called tubular weaving, creative knitting, or spool knitting. It is an innovative approach to what many of us did as children, using four nails and a spool to make a long tubular braid, which we worked into pot holders, place mats, or rugs. Estelle Carlson uses an innovative method of stiffening the spidery web-like form with clear plastic casting resin (such as Clear Cast or Crystal Cast), as shown in the illustrations. After several coats are applied and the form is self-supporting, she sprays it with paints. The sculpture is weatherproof, so it can stay outside; but it is lightweight, so it must be weighted.

PHOTO SERIES: COURTESY, ARTIST

(a) After the netting has been woven, it is anchored by the frame in which it was made, and strings suspend it at the top. Pieces of foam rubber are placed inside to create the shape desired. Some parts are tied together. Then it is painted with the four coats of casting resin, which reacts with the fibers to make them hard.

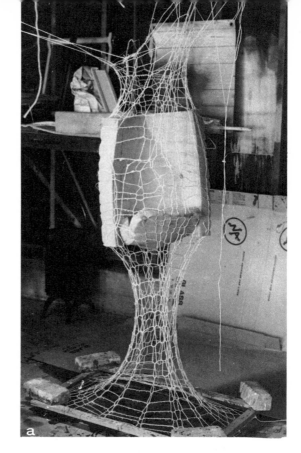

(b) The pads are removed, but the support strings are left in place. Additional coats of casting resin are applied until the piece is self-supporting.

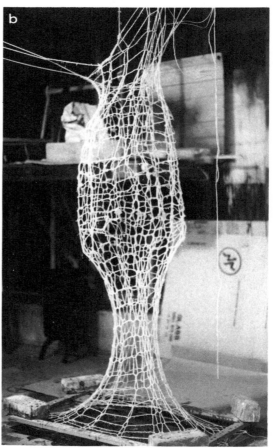

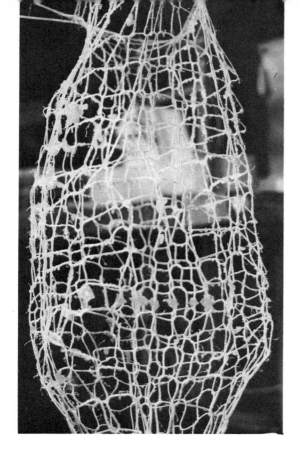

(c) Final build-up shows the casting resin's appearance as a colorless solid on some of the fibers.

(d) The final shape may be spray painted. It is completely self-supporting, but because it weighs only three pounds, it must be weighted.

SCULPTURE. Estelle Carlson.

A picture frame or a piece of wood with a shape cut out may be
used for tubular knitting. Place nails or pegs at various intervals
about ½ inch from the edge of the circle or frame. Start yarn by
wrapping loosely around pegs. For the second row and all other
rows hold the yarn around the pegs and lift the lower loop over the
yarn and over the top of the peg with a crochet hook or pointed
instrument such as an awl or a rug hook. Continue to
make these forms as large or as small as you like. Estelle Carlson
works with pegs far apart to result in loose, spidery forms.
Sharon La Pierre places pegs closer together to knit forms that
are then incorporated into a tubular weaving. The entire weaving
can be made with this method.

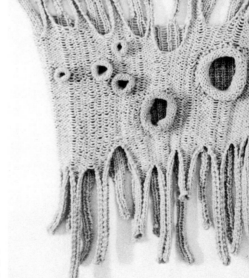

TUBULAR WEAVING.
Sharon La Pierre. Jute twine. 32 inches high, 36 inches
wide. A large portion is constructed on a frame; then the
portion is removed and placed on a dowel. Small tubular
shapes are knitted separately and added on later.

KNITTED HANGING SCULPTURE.
Estelle Carlson. Fuzzy nylon yarn
worked with round knitting needles
and mounted on wire hoops.
Combinations of a stockinette and
knit stitch are used. The sculpture
was sprayed with plastic resin so
that it could be hung outdoors
without deteriorating from the
weather. 3½ feet long and 28 inches
at the widest part.

Knitted sculpture is worked in the
same manner as knitting a skirt.
Form shapes by use of different
stitch combinations, by increasing
and decreasing as necessary, and by
the use of wire hoops.

PHOTOS: COURTESY, ESTELLE CARLSON

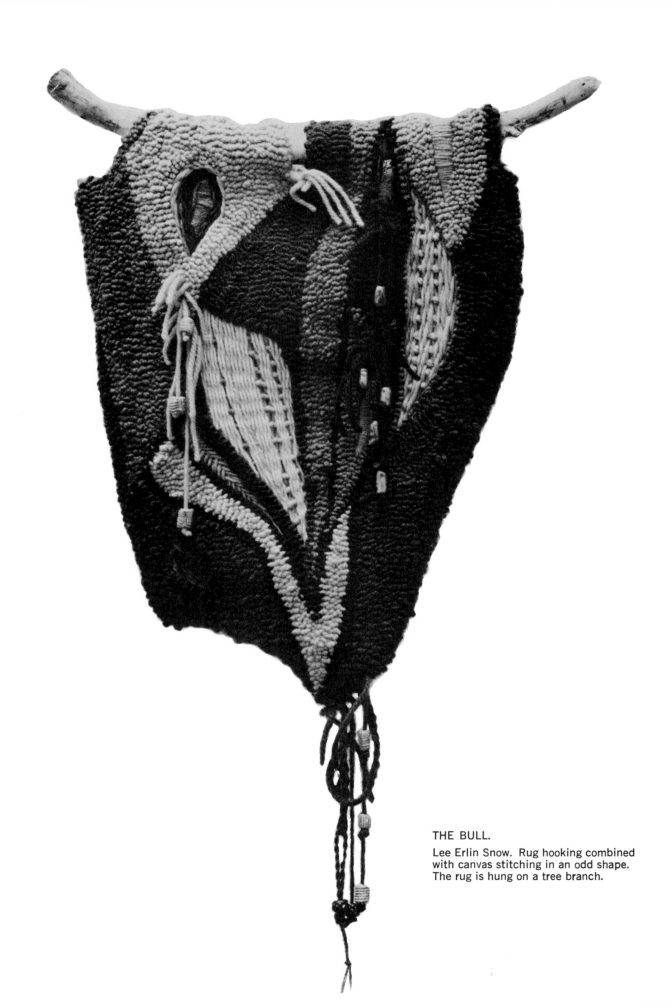

THE BULL.

Lee Erlin Snow. Rug hooking combined
with canvas stitching in an odd shape.
The rug is hung on a tree branch.

rugmaking

The history of rugs is rich. It includes the seventeenth- and eighteenth-century pieces found throughout France and Spain, which record many historical events, such as the coronation of Napoleon. There are early American hooked rugs with traditional, often repeated patterns. Eventually the handmade rug gave way to industrialization, and floor rugs were no longer considered great works of art. Today, however, the resurgence of the well-designed rug has once again captured the talent and imagination of crafts-men and is rapidly taking its own place among the textile arts.

Explosive colors and dramatically different patterns appeared in the early 1960s in the revival of the rya rug, from Scandinavia. The highly textured, durable yarn pieces were so beautiful that many people began to display the rugs on their walls as well as on their floors. Little by little, craftsmen began to use the old rughooking methods and then the newer, faster rugpunching technique to push yarns through a backing. It was only a short time

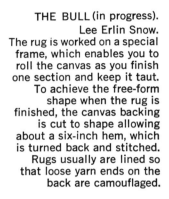

THE BULL (in progress).
Lee Erlin Snow.
The rug is worked on a special
frame, which enables you to
roll the canvas as you finish
one section and keep it taut.
To achieve the free-form
shape when the rug is
finished, the canvas backing
is cut to shape allowing
about a six-inch hem, which
is turned back and stitched.
Rugs usually are lined so
that loose yarn ends on the
back are camouflaged.

before rugmakers began to solve the same problems in textiles that the painter must solve in creating his designs using paint. But the rugmaker had two additional problems: that of texture and an added dimension due to the raised surface area of the yarns. Soon rugmakers began to abandon the practice of cutting yarn heights evenly, and rugs began to have multi-leveled areas. Sometimes yarns were inches and even feet longer than the background yarns.

Rugmaking caught on along with other textile arts perhaps because of the tremendous variety and colors of natural and synthetic fibers that could be worked into many types of backing material. The ease with which some of the new tools manufactured for the craftsmen are worked also is greatly responsible for the interest in textile arts. The challenge of using many kinds of techniques is irresistible to many artists who combine rugmaking with wrapping, macramé, and weaving, and often add shells, buttons, beads, and other objects to enrich the surface of the work.

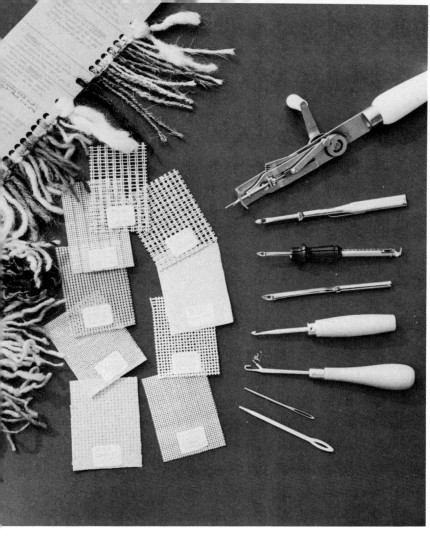

Materials for rugmaking include the yarns and cords (sample cords such as these are available from sources listed in the back of the book). Many rugmaking yarns are available from craft and needle-work suppliers. The closeness of the weave and the material used for backing materials differ. Looser weaves may be used for thick yarns; closer weaves are used for thinner yarns. An assortment of rugmaking tools is shown. Top to bottom: automatic rugpunch, three hand manipulated rug punches, rug hook, latchet hook, and needles.

There are three basic methods of attaching fibers through rug backing: hooking, punching, or sewing with a needle. The surface yarn may be a cut pile or a loop or a combination of both.

To design a rug, you can work out a pattern on paper and transfer the design to the backing material with a waterproof pen. Colors may be indicated directly on the canvas by lettering each panel or by actually painting color on areas with a thin solution of acrylic paint. By painting the colors directly onto the backing you will have some idea of color relationship and you will be sure that you have plotted your color areas properly. Select the colors and hues of yarns that look good together while they are still in the skeins. Select the proper backing for the needle and yarn you are using (too loose a weave will cause yarns to pull out). The weave must be close enough to hold the particular thickness of yarn without its slipping out. If you use too tight a woven backing for the yarn thickness, it will be difficult to pass the fibers through the holes.

RUGMAKING   LATCHET HOOKING.

Latchet hooking uses precut lengths of yarn. Each piece of yarn is individually placed around the needle, through the backing and knotted; the result is always a cut pile, as opposed to a loop pile. Latchet hooking is not so fast a technique as punching; the main advantage is that if one piece of yarn loosens, it in no way affects the others because each piece is individually knotted into the backing. For latchet hooking you need a special mesh backing with four holes per inch to allow the hook to penetrate the material.

(a) The hook is placed in one hole and brought up through the hole above it with the movable latch part placed as shown. The yarn is folded in half and placed over the shank of the hook.

(b) Wind both ends of yarn over the latch device and under the hook and bring it to the left side.

(c) Pull the hook toward you until the latch falls forward and begins to close; this step automatically locks the stitch. Let go of the loose ends and continue to pull the yarn through. Remove the hook and pull the knot tight with your finger.

(d) Continue filling each hole for the entire row. Use the next pair of holes for each subsequent row. Various lengths of yarn may be trimmed to any height desired.

a   b   c

Fibers mentioned in previous chapters can be used for rugmaking as long as they fit through the rughooking tool and backing. To facilitate some punching and hooking techniques the backing material should be held taut in a rughooking frame or stapled to a picture frame or canvas stretcher. For large rugs simply move the portions to be worked along the frame as you progress. Latchet hooking and rya are worked without a frame.

As you study the examples of rugs shown here, it will be difficult to determine which tool was used for each piece. So far as the finished item is concerned, it is the statement that is most important, not how it was done. Almost any result can be achieved with any tool you choose to work with. However, the latchet hook can be used for a cut pile only. Hooking, punching, and rya techniques are worked as loops but may be cut for varying effects. All of these techniques may be worked at several heights and used with other techniques such as macrame, needlepoint, etc.

PUNCHING.

There are several types of rug-punching tools available. Illustrated is
the Columbia-Minerva punch, which is versatile and easy to use. The
principle involved is that the yarn feeds through the needle by way of a slot.
The punch is poked through closely woven burlap or linen backing and
lifted just to the top of the fabric. As the needle is pulled up, a loop half
the length of the shank is formed. Multiple loops are made by simply punching
the needle up and down in rows. This particular needle may be adjusted for
six different height loops; there are two shanks for use with thin or thick
cord. Multiple-looped punched rugs can be damaged; if one loop is pulled,
several may come out. However, latex rug backing can be brushed on the
back to secure the yarns. Hooked rugs always are worked from the back so
that the pattern on the front is reversed.

AUTOMATIC RUG PUNCH.

An automatic rug punch works very much like an egg beater. It is
adjustable to three heights, but it will accommodate only yarns that are
no thicker than a knitting worsted. The tool is exceptionally efficient.
For all punching the backing must be held taut by stapling or tacking
it to a frame.

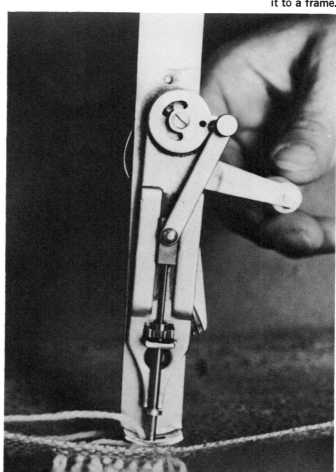

CITYSCAPE.
Jay Hinz. Persian yarns worked with the punching method.
18 inches high, 48 inches wide.

"CARTOON," OR DRAWING FOR *CITYSCAPE.*
Observe that the finished rug is actually the reverse of
the drawing. In punching you work from the back of the
rug; the finished looping appears on the side opposite
that on which the cartoon is drawn.

90

WAVES.
(Detail). Henry Stahmer. Shapes are drawn on burlap, and hooked areas result in the raised portion. The flat areas are shapes of leather glued directly to the backing.

FIGURE.
Bill Hinz. Muted tones of grays and browns. 36 inches square.

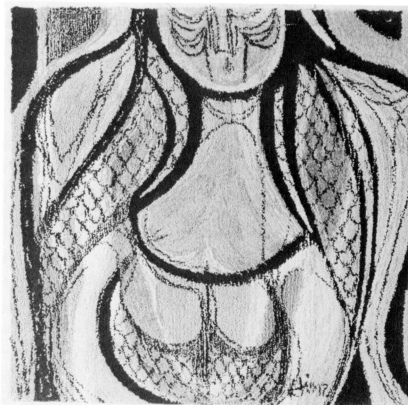

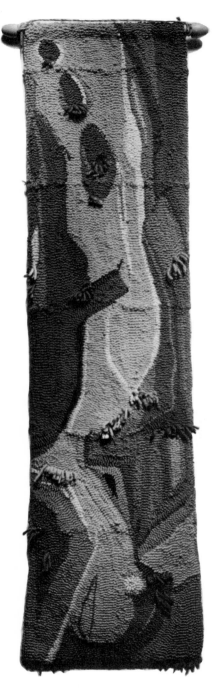

RED RUG.
Lee Erlin Snow. Loops are of different heights. Some have been made very long and snipped so that loose ends move throughout the design.
PHOTO: BOB LOPEZ

PITTSBURGH.
Hildegarde Klene. After a drawing by José Bermudez in dark gray, blue, and gold wool yarn. 60 inches high, 42 inches wide.
PHOTO: JOSÉ BERMUDEZ

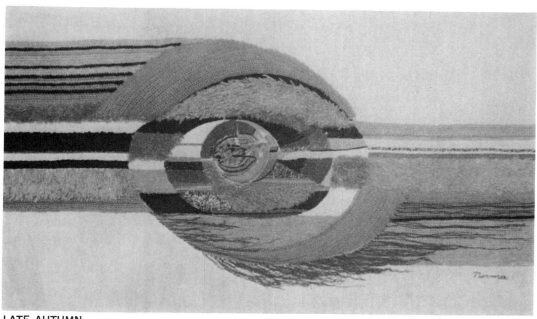

LATE AUTUMN.

Norma C. Minkowitz. Many techniques may be successfully combined. Composed of 4-ply wool knitting worsted, the hooked, stitched, and stuffed crochet panels are used for this design, which is worked on a background of velvet.

COURTESY: ARTIST

ABSTRACT.

Estelle Rothstein. Wool fabrics stripped and hooked into burlap. 3 feet high, 6 feet, 4 inches wide.

COURTESY: ARTIST

RUGMAKING

Traute Ishida uses the latchet hook for her huge compositions, which are mounted on wood that has been cut to the necessary shape. Latchet hooking (see page 88) is accomplished through a special loosely woven backing available in department store needlework sections. It is usually worked with short lengths of yarn knotted through the backing with the hook. You work from the right side, and the result is a cut pile rather than the loop pile. However, Mrs. Ishida also hooks with longer pieces of wool in bundles and braids and may sometimes simply fasten groups of wool to the front.

PHOTOS: COURTESY, ARTIST

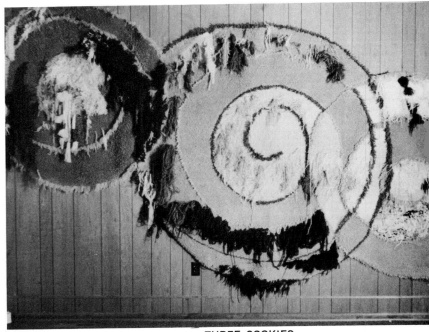

THREE COOKIES.
Traute Ishida. Yarns of various types and colors are worked with pile.

ONE RAINDROP.
Traute Ishida.

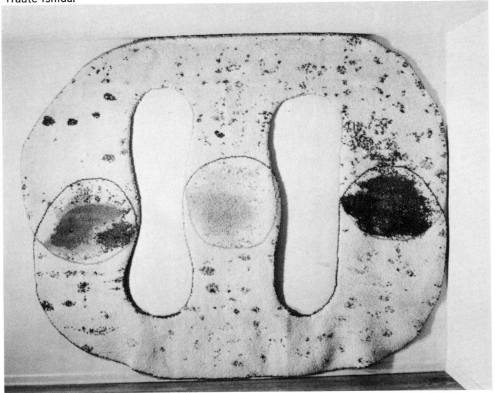

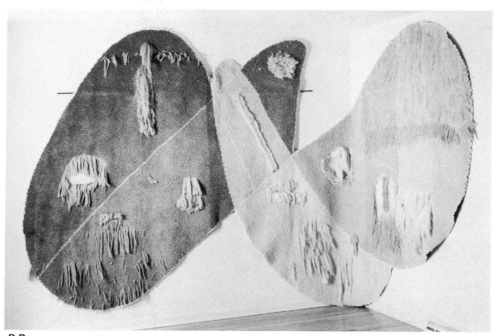

R.R.
Traute Ishida.

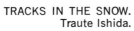

TRACKS IN THE SNOW.
Traute Ishida.

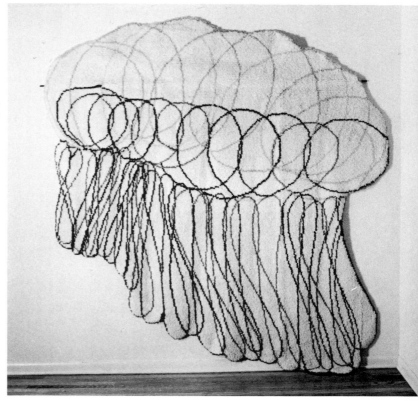

EQUATOR.
Gloria F. Ross and Morris Leurs.
Hooked wool. 63 inches square.
COURTESY: RICHARD FEIGEN GALLERY, NEW YORK

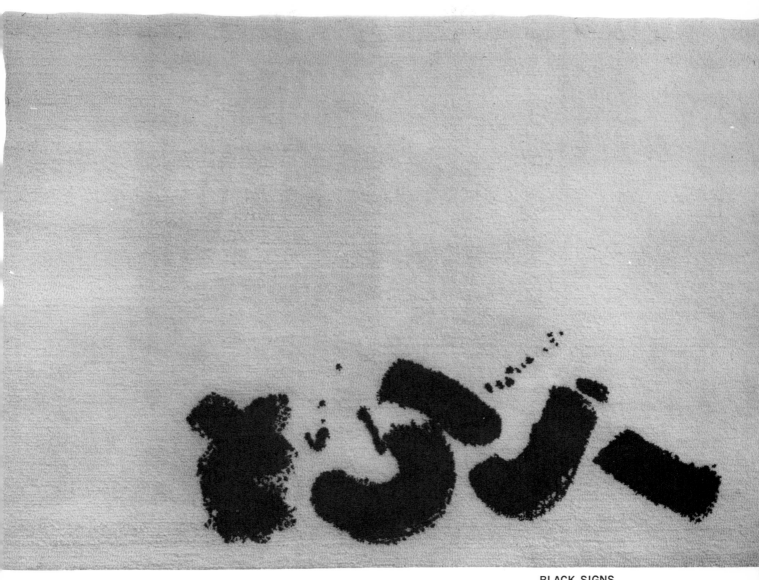

BLACK SIGNS.
Gloria F. Ross and Adolph Gottlieb. Hooked
wool. 4½ feet high, 6 feet wide.
COURTESY: RICHARD FEIGEN GALLERY, NEW YORK

WINTERDRAWING.
(Detail). Hildegarde Klene.
Hooked wool.
PHOTO: JOSÉ BERMUDEZ.

97

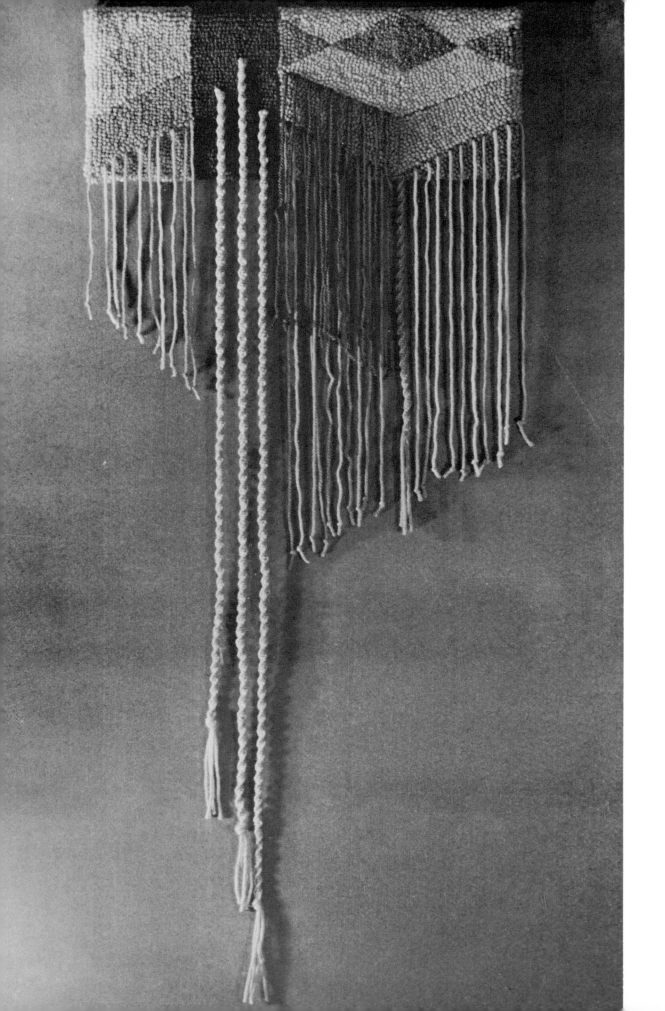

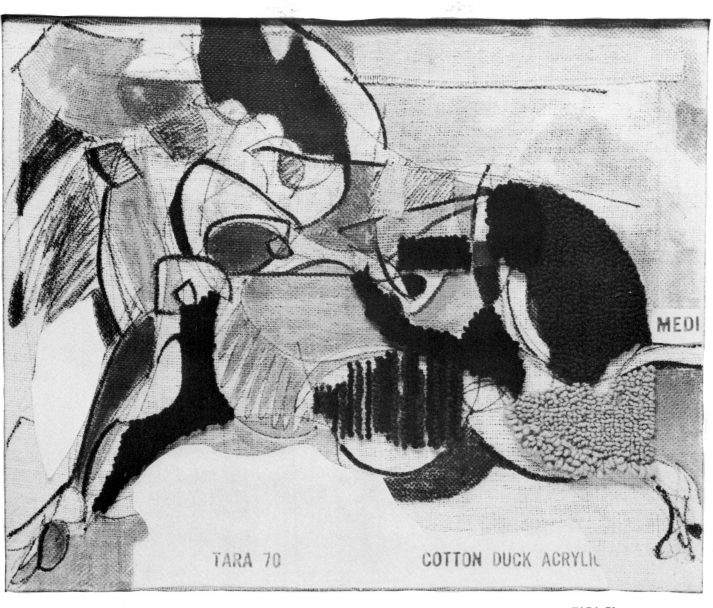

TARA 70.
Suzanne Gertz. Collage, painting, drawing, and rughooking.

RED DIAMOND *(opposite page).*
Hildegarde Klene. Wool in shades of red and dark blue
with macramé half knot twist sennits.

FLOWERS AND BIRDS (top).
Eva Ludwig. Hooked room divider. In hooking;
many loose ends normally appear on the back
of the work. However, Eva Ludwig has pulled
loose yarn ends through and cut them the same
height as the pile. Her work is so neat that she
has created a room divider that has both
hooking and the backs of stitches on each side.
Front and back are, of course, reversed.

COURTESY: ARTIST

FLOWERS AND BIRDS (left).
(Detail, back). The pattern is reversed. The
stitches are so carefully punched that the
flat areas could be mistaken for crewel work.

RYA WALL HANGING.
Estelle Carlson. Rya yarn may be
used with a latchet hook or with a
rya stitch worked with a needle. The
loop can be short or very long,
depending on the desired effect.
Loops usually are cut for long hanging
cut pile and texture.

COURTESY: ARTIST

WALL HANGING.
Traute Ishida. Yellow
center with blue at the bottom,
blue and orange at the top.

COURTESY: ARTIST

IKAT WEAVING.
Karen Chang. Loosely woven fibers are combined with a stitched fabric border with beads added to both border and weaving. Ikat is a Javanese term that refers to the practice of dying the fibers of the warp in a method similar to the tie-dye technique. The fabric border is tie-dyed, and the fibers are worked in to match the borders. Sometimes dyes are applied directly to the fibers just before they are woven.

weaving

Weaving has traditionally been accomplished on some kind of loom. Threads stretched lengthwise are called the warp. Other threads are crossed under and over the warp, and these are called the weft, or filler. The manner in which the warp and weft interlock results in the weave.

Most of us are accustomed to woven fabrics that have warp and weft threads that have been worked to create tight weaves for clothing and other useful items. We assume that these fabrics are woven on conventional wooden looms or on machines associated with the industrial weaving of fabrics. Of course, all this is true.

However, as artists have applied new thinking to uses for fibers and fabrics, weaving too has been subject to tremendous experimentation; the impressive results have widespread interest for craftsmen. In addition to loom weaving you can weave on what have been termed "non-looms."

A picture frame can be used for weaving. Warp twine around the frame evenly, as shown. Weave a weft yarn at the top and bottom and tie the yarn around the sides of the frame to pull the layers together. This will make weaving easier. Weaving is accomplished with a large plastic needle. The weft must be pushed into place with the teeth of a comb. For small pieces a frame, such as the holder from drapery trim, may be improvised.

What is non-loom weaving? Essentially it is weaving without the usual wood loom, with its pedals and shuttles. Instead an improvised structure is used on which you can string a warp and work the crosswise weft over and under, using your fingers, a shuttle, a bobbin, a needle, or any item that will pull the thread through. You might think of the pot holders that most of us wove when we were children, in which the warp and weft were attached to nails driven into a frame. The non-loom may consist simply of a picture frame, a piece of masonite with a strip of molding at the top and bottom to hold the thread above the wood surface, a wheel (or other circular form), or simply the branch of a tree.

Working on a non-loom can result in a rigid pattern similar to those woven on a standard upright loom. However, non-loom weaving enables you to depart radically from traditional weaving techniques because it encourages an open, unstructured weaving design. Weaves worked on a non-loom are often very loose and

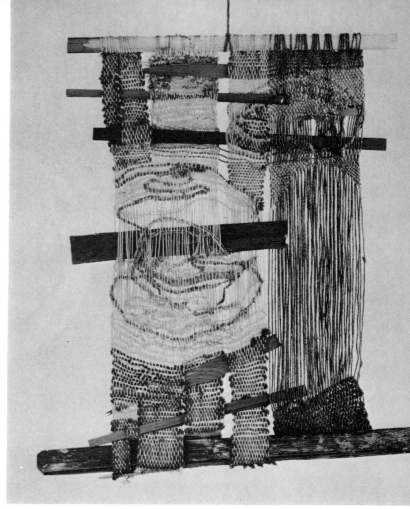

asymmetrical, and there may be large open areas with several strands of the warp tied off. There may be odd shapes, padded areas, and combinations of weaving with other techniques such as braiding, macrame, and stitchery. The fascinating possibilities are infinite.

Along with the yarns and warps used for weaving, many other materials such as pieces of wood, metal, leather strips, feathers, raffia, Swistraw, and springs may be used for the weft.

This chapter does not attempt to teach traditional weaving; rather, it encourages you to warp any kind of frame or object and to begin to weave in and out, using assorted threads, yarns, or cords to develop designs. In all the accompanying examples the technique is not so important as the result; the craftsman, not the technique, must control the work. Technique is simply the method used to arrive at a finished statement.

A simple board for weaving is made from a rectangle of masonite with grooves cut evenly at both ends to hold the warp straight *(top).* A piece of molding is glued about ¼ inch from each end to hold the warp above the board. The warp is wound by taping the first cord at the back of the board and then winding. Weaving is done with a large needle.

Here the front level of the warp is being woven. The back layer may be woven later for another dimension, or it may be cut and used to provide an unusual bottom and top treatment.

NON-LOOM WEAVING (Detail). Virginia Black. Raffia or straw and pieces of wood are woven through the warp of different colors and thicknesses of yarn.

COURTESY: ARTIST

WEAVING. Lee Erlin Snow. Weaving accomplished on the board may be removed and placed on a branch or other object. Any loose warp and weft cords can be developed into many arrangements using frazzled ends, braiding, wrapping, and beads.

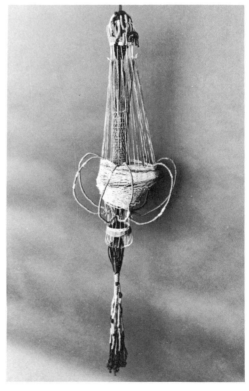

BEEHIVE.
Pat Baldwin. A gutter guard and wrapped wires serve as the warp for wool, rayon, chenille, and jute weft in a three-dimension sculpture. 48 inches long, 18 inches in diameter.

COURTESY: ARTIST

WEAVING

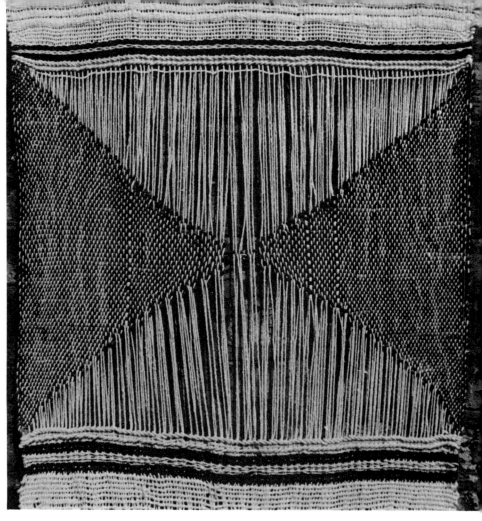

Detail of the kind of weave possible when you use a simple frame weaving technique. By beginning students at the Barb Pleason Weaving Workshop, Chicago.

PHOTOS: TRUDY SCHRAGLE

WEAVING IN A FRAME.

Roberta Harmon. Panel of
leather laid over the warps
and wefts. Other woven
materials include raw wool,
leather strips, rawhide, rope,
horsehair, ceramic, and bone
pieces. 6 feet high, 3 feet
wide.

109

WEAVING

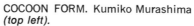

COCOON FORM. Kumiko Murashima *(top left).*
Weaving through a shaped wire screen.
50 inches long, 10 inches in diameter.

WEAVING WITH PADDED SECTION *(top right).*
Virginia Tiffany. This piece may be used as a hanging or as a room divider.

PHOTOGRAPHED AT ART INDEPENDENT, LAKE GENEVA, WISCONSIN

PORTRAIT *(bottom).*
Virginia Bock.
Frame weaving with holes drilled through frame molding to hold warp and weft.

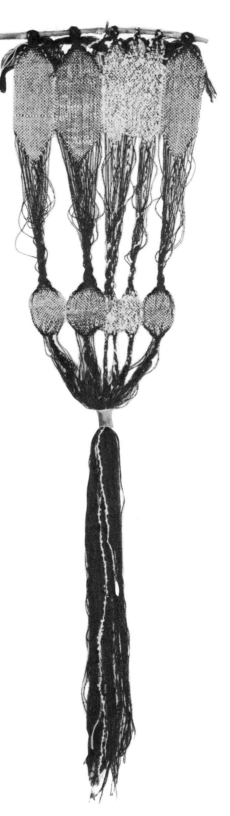

BANNER #2.
Mary B. Buskirk. Wool, linen, and eucalyptus.
31 inches high, 8½ inches wide.
COURTESY: ARTIST

JUGGLER.
Berni Gorski. A combination of sweater, glove, sock stretchers, and hoop. This lace weaving technique is composed of black yarn and threads with some plastic for the solid sections in the head.
COURTESY: ARTIST

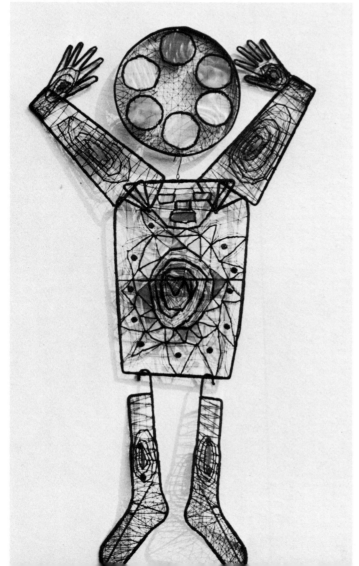

111

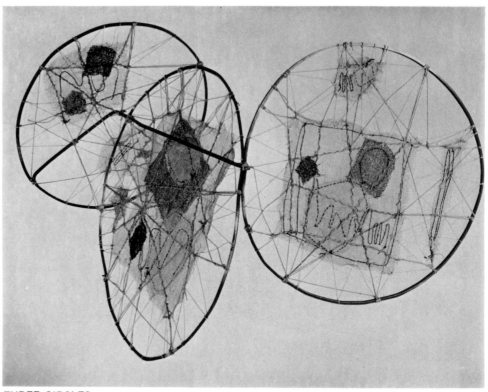

THREE CIRCLES.
Winifred Roth. Welded metal
hoops connected with a rod are
used for the weaving "loom."
PHOTO: JAMES COURSEY

SCULPTURAL WEAVING.
Pat Baldwin. Acrylic cylinders woven in
one and two planes with wool, linen,
cotton, acrylics, and monofilament.
COURTESY: ARTIST

CREATURE WITH FUR.
Winifred Roth.
PHOTO: JAMES COURSEY

WEAVING IN WRAPPED WHEEL.
Student, Design West, Los Angeles, 1970.

BARREL HOOP WEAVING.
Bici Linklater.
Jute and sisal with
rusty bolts and springs.
COURTESY: ARTIST

113

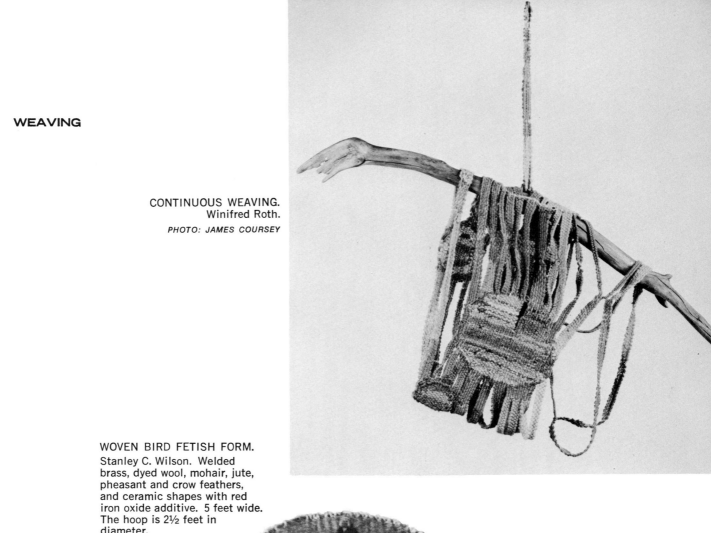

CONTINUOUS WEAVING.
Winifred Roth.
PHOTO: JAMES COURSEY

WOVEN BIRD FETISH FORM.
Stanley C. Wilson. Welded
brass, dyed wool, mohair, jute,
pheasant and crow feathers,
and ceramic shapes with red
iron oxide additive. 5 feet wide.
The hoop is 2½ feet in
diameter.
COURTESY: ARTIST

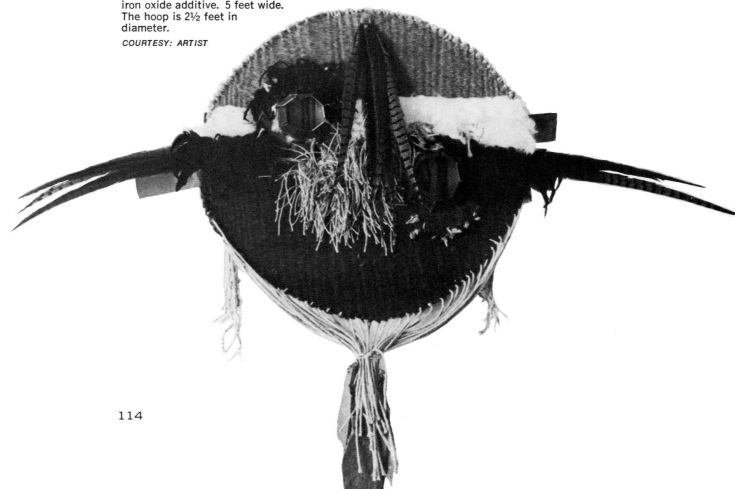

114

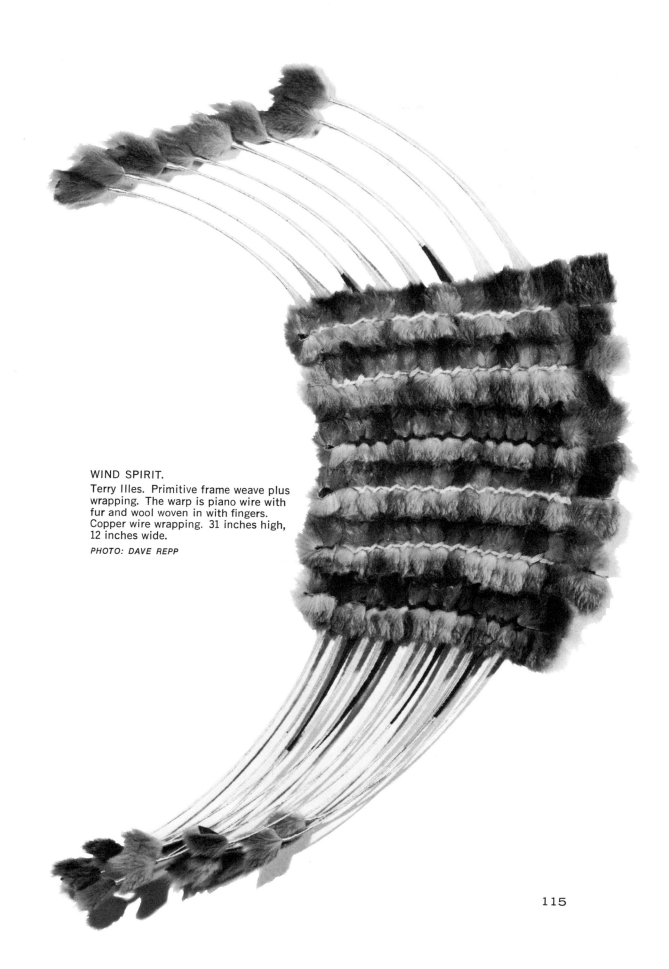

WIND SPIRIT.
Terry Illes. Primitive frame weave plus wrapping. The warp is piano wire with fur and wool woven in with fingers. Copper wire wrapping. 31 inches high, 12 inches wide.

PHOTO: DAVE REPP

FABRIC COLLAGE.
Ronald Rolfe. Unusual effects can be achieved when fabrics dipped
in a polymer medium are treated with concentrated water colors
(see demonstration on pages 120-121).

COLLECTION: DONA MEILACH

collage
and appliqué

It may seem unorthodox to combine collage and appliqué because they are derived from such different uses. But in today's "anything goes" approach to creativity, the two techniques overlap and coexist.

The word collage is derived from the French word *coller,* meaning "to paste." Collage appeared as an art form in the early 1900s when Pablo Picasso and Georges Braque pasted objects onto a painted canvas. Early collage work is associated with the use of paper, but it has rapidly broadened to encompass the pasting of materials such as cloth, metal, wood, and a limitless assortment of found objects onto a canvas.

Appliqué also is a French word, and it refers to "applied work," in which one material is "laid on" another. However, applied work has a long history, which, as a method for decorating fabrics, dates back to early Egyptian and Greek civilizations.

COLLAGE
AND APPLIQUÉ

DOUBLE FABRIC COLLAGE.
Ronald Rolfe. Two separate rectangular
compositions are mounted on one board beneath
black matte board and framed. Black lines are
carefully drawn after the fabrics have dried.

FABRIC COLLAGE.
Ronald Rolfe. Fabrics bled with color are mounted
beneath a black felt circle and framed. A circular
grid of strung gold wire over nails adds a relief
dimension.
COLLECTION: DONA MEILACH

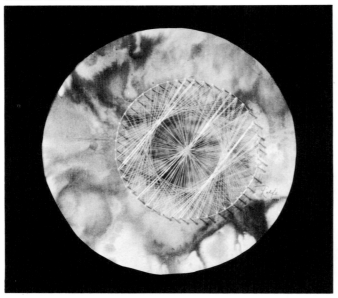

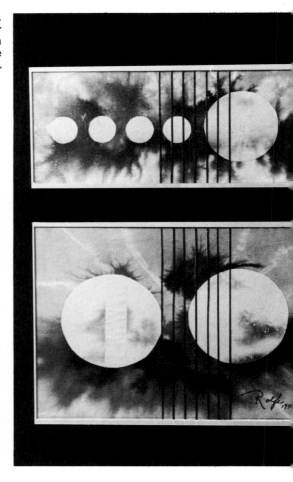

Throughout the years appliqué has been associated with needlework, but many fabrics were also pasted, and padding was often placed between the fabrics for a raised effect.

The contemporary artist uses fabrics and fibers on a painter's canvas and may use collage or appliqué alone or in combination with other methods. Ronald Rolfe and Elvie Ten Hoor use fabrics with modern acrylic paints and water colors to create new statements.

Polymer media, recent chemical discoveries, have proved valuable to the collage-appliqué artist because they simultaneously adhere to a surface and harden it without changing its texture, color, or pattern. Polymers are applied with a brush, and they dry transparent and hard in about an hour.

MOON BIRTH.
Elisabet Siewert-Miller. Textured and smooth fabrics
carefully appliquéd. 45 inches high, 23 inches wide.
PHOTO: NICKERSON

FABRIC COLLAGE TECHNIQUE DEMONSTRATED BY RONALD ROLFE.

(a) Materials include a masonite board, gesso, polymer gel medium, fabrics, scissors, paintbrushes, and coloring such as dyes, inks, acrylic paints, and concentrated water colors. Fabrics may be cotton percales and silks you tie-dye yourself. Do not use permanent press and synthetic fabrics because they don't absorb inks and watercolors satisfactorily. Use 100 percent cotton, silk, or linen.

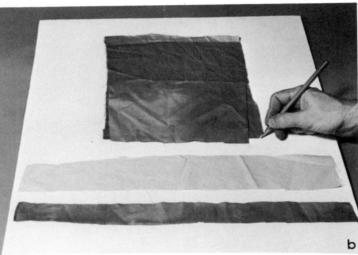

(b) Coat board with gesso and let dry. Plan the layout of fabrics on the dry board, placing one color over another and cutting circles in the fabrics to allow an undercolor to come through. Mark the fabric placement lightly with a pencil. Once the fabrics and the board are wet, you must work quickly.

(c) Soak fabrics in water for a few minutes. Fabrics must be wet so that they will absorb the dye colors and allow them to bleed.

(d) While the fabric is soaking, cover the board with a coat of gloss polymer gel medium. Dilute one quart of gloss medium with seven tablespoons hot water.

120

(e) Place wet fabric (slightly wrung out) on wet polymer-coated board. The polymer acts as a glue, causing the fabric to adhere to it. Apply another coat of gel medium over the fabric, brushing material from the center out to remove air bubbles. Repeat with the second and third layers of fabric, always working quickly while the board and the fabric are wet.

(f) Begin to drip the coloring on the wet fabrics so that they will bleed in abstract designs. Gently splattered on the fabric, water color concentrate, ink, and fabric dyes will spread through the fibers in seconds.

(g) Other effects may be achieved by dropping colors onto the fabric with an eyedropper.

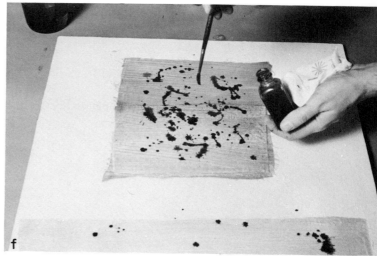

(h) For a denser effect color may be brushed on lightly. After fabric is dry, you can revise the effect anywhere you like by rewetting the fabric with gesso and bleeding color into it. Spots may be added to colored areas with gesso.

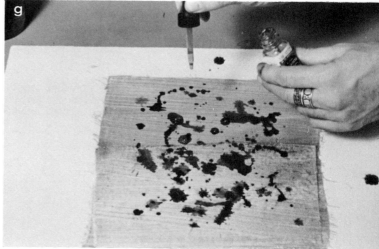

A fabric relief collage may be built up with many
materials. Elvie Ten Hoor uses polymer gel medium
to attach fabrics and fibers but builds up solid
relief shapes with modeled instant papier mâché,
which dries hard and accepts polymers.
After the pieces of fabric had been cut and attached,
certain areas were built up with papier mâché.

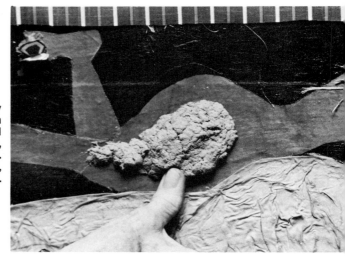

Satin is pinned in place and draped.

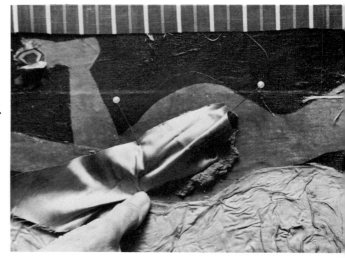

Full-strength polymer gel is brushed over the fabric.
The gel penetrates the fabric, attaches it to the
board, and hardens it.

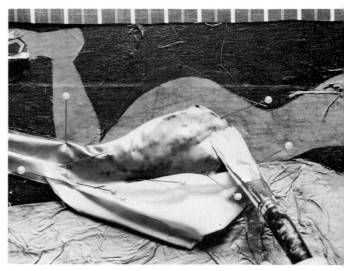

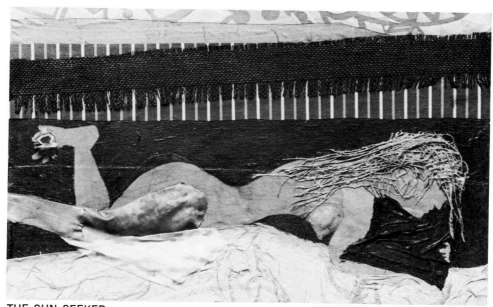

THE SUN SEEKER.
Elvie Ten Hoor. Smooth bronze satin on the padded nude
body contrasts with the textured and patterned fabrics.

THE GARDENER.
Elvie Ten Hoor. Fabric-stuffed glove hardened with polymer.
Paper rose and tree. Fabric leaves in flat and relief shapes.
Polymer gel attaches and holds the shapes.

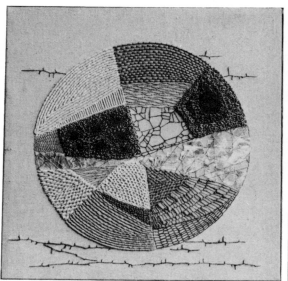

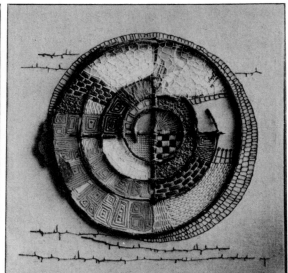

COMPOSITION.
Virginia Tiffany. Metal, paper, mica sewn and glued onto blue
linen with stitchery. 18 inches high, 40 inches wide.
PHOTOGRAPHED AT ART INDEPENDENT, LAKE GENEVA, WISCONSIN

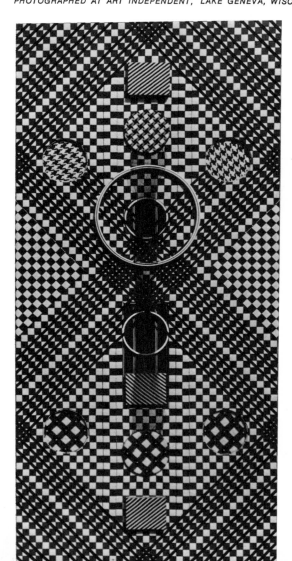

BLACK AND WHITE #2.
Susan H. Brown. Fabrics
arranged in concave and convex
areas and mounted in a shadow
box form.
COURTESY: ARTIST

KNIT HANGING
(opposite page).
Jane Knight.
PHOTO: RICHARD KNIGHT

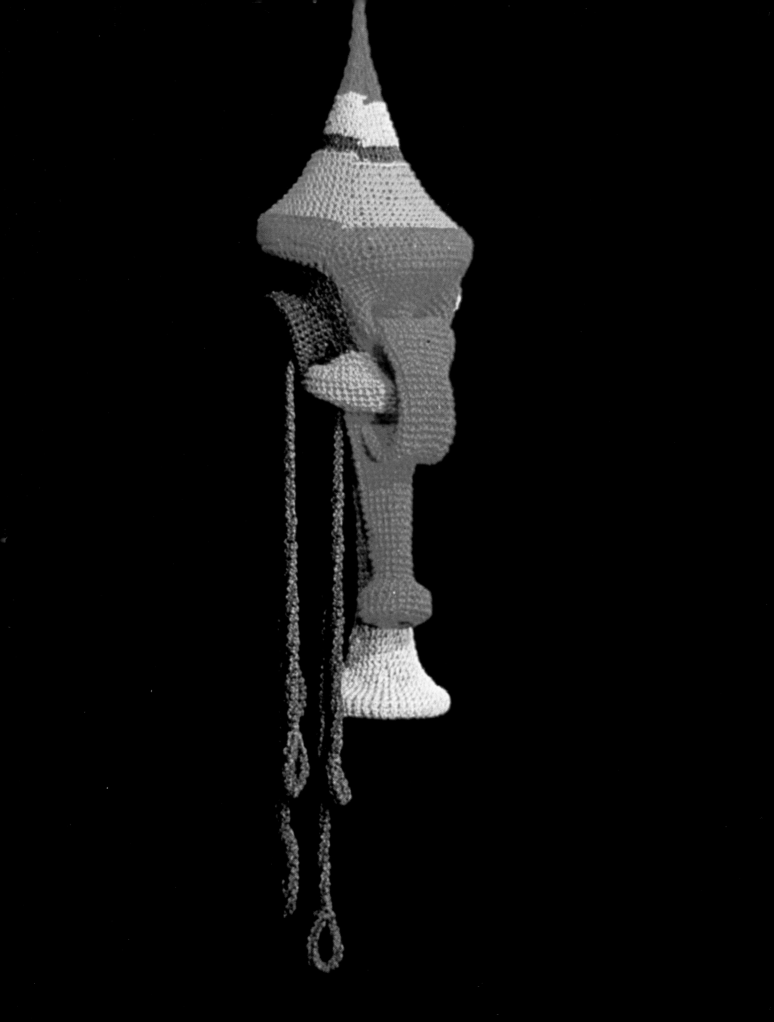

MABEL RAINBOW.
Deborah Frederick.
Wrapping. 41 inches high,
26 inches wide.

TEMPLE. Deborah Frederick.
Knotting, wrapping, crochet.
17 inches high, 7 inches wide.
COURTESY: ARTIST

126

GUERNICA.
Enrico Baj. 141 inches high,
307 inches wide. Acrylic and
collage on tapestry.
COURTESY: MUSEUM OF
CONTEMPORARY ART, CHICAGO

WALL SCULPTURE.
Jane Knight. Wrapping.
PHOTO: RICHARD KNIGHT

PATCHWORK HANGING.
Sas Colby.
PHOTO: DONA MEILACH

127

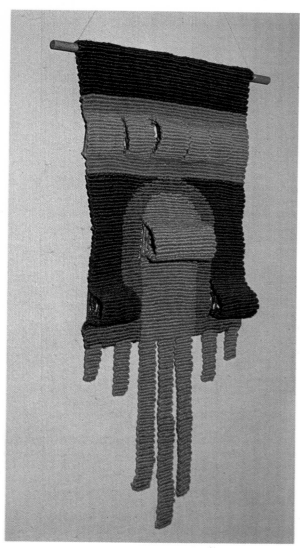

SMALL TOWN IN MY DREAMS
(top left). Michi Ouchi. Macramé.
42 inches high, 18 inches wide.
COURTESY: ARTIST

CARL'S CAKE (top right).
Marilyn Leon. Crochet.
PHOTO: JIM ZIMMERMAN

TOWER (bottom right).
Joan Michaels Paque. Macramé and
other knotting techniques on wire hoops.
PHOTO: MEL MEILACH

RING AROUND (opposite page).
Stana Coleman. Knitting rake
is warped and woven; stuffed
knitted heads are stitched to weaving.
PHOTO: DONA MEILACH

FIRE HYDRANT.
Sally Davidson. Macramé with jute.
PHOTO: DONA MEILACH

YE OLDE AUTOMOBILE. Kathleen
Knippel. Stuffed soft sculpture.
COURTESY: ARTIST

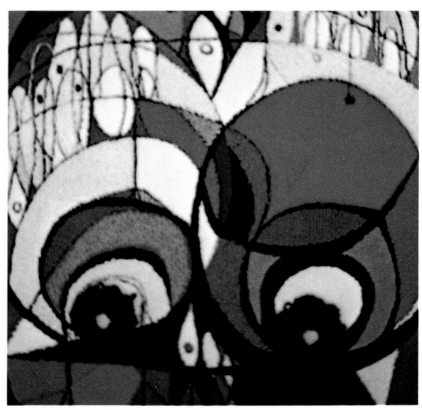

UNTITLED. Jay and Bill Hinz. Hooked rug hanging.
COURTESY: ARTISTS

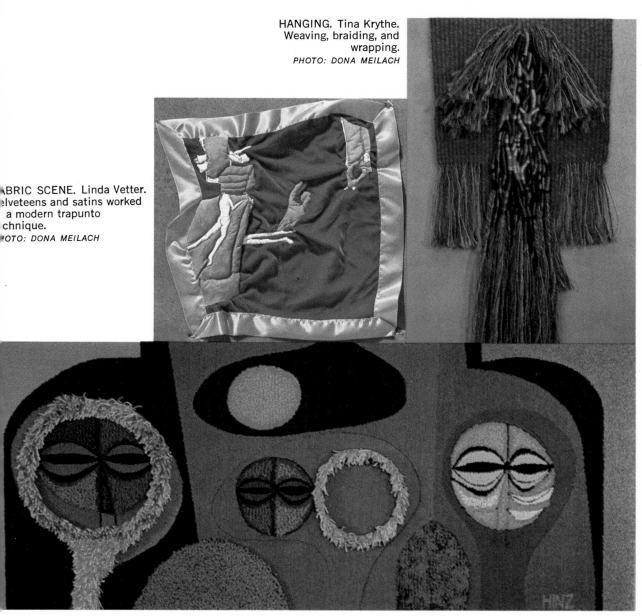

HANGING. Tina Krythe.
Weaving, braiding, and
wrapping.
PHOTO: DONA MEILACH

ABRIC SCENE. Linda Vetter.
elveteens and satins worked
a modern trapunto
chnique.
OTO: DONA MEILACH

UNTITLED. Jay and Bill Hinz. Hooked rug hanging.
COURTESY: ARTISTS

SCULPTURE. Estelle Carlson.
Spool weaving stiffened with acrylic resin. *COURTESY: ARTIST*

ROPE.
Nancy J. Koehler. Manila
rope on acrylic-painted
canvas. 144 inches long, 12
to 30 inches wide.
COURTESY: ARTIST

FIGURES.
Wilcke Smith. Padded
appliqué with stitchery.
COURTESY: ARTIST

PRIMITIVE.
Claude Bentley. Fabric,
wood, and found objects.

COLLAGE.
Ruben Steinberg. Leather and rope glued and tacked.

RENAISSANCE.
Sas Colby. Patchwork hanging with designed fabric, crochet, and lace over patterned materials. The black strips at the top are actually open areas. The colored lining shows through the lacework.

patchwork

If the word "patchwork" conjures pictures of little ladies with glasses on their noses, laboriously blindstitching random patches for quilts to ward off the chill, you've been reading your needlework history books. Patchwork does date back to early European and American cultures, in which no scrap of material was wasted.

Another image that you might have of patchwork is the crazy quilt. The crazy quilt was the result of random repair of holes in pants and skirts, and it led to entire fabrics made of patches sewn together in any haphazard manner.

But today's artist has carried patchwork out of the homemaker's realm and into the art classroom and studio. Many patchwork examples by modern artists have been created as wall hangings as well as coverings, but the manner in which the patches are used is as carefully planned and controlled as if the artist were using paint and palette.

TEXAS.
Rhonda Ronan. Patchwork sheepskin extends
7 feet along the floor and climbs the wall for 3 feet.
*PHOTOGRAPHED ON EXHIBIT AT THE ART
INSTITUTE OF CHICAGO.*

The purist patchworker usually emulates designs, using triangles, hexagons, and other shapes that were used by our ancestors. He cuts these shapes with templates and sews them with tiny hand stitches. The modern patchworker will mix shapes and fabrics and often will have the stitches so large that they become part of the overall design. In addition, a patchwork hanging may not even be a solid shape; rather, it may have negative areas as part of the design. Patchwork also may be used pictorially, as in the examples by Pat and Foster Marlow.

Modern fabrics, glues, and adhesive backings also simplify the patchwork process. Patches usually are easier to handle when they are lightly stiffened with a coat of water base glue, which will wash out, or when they are made from presized fabrics. Spray sizing also is used for stiffening patchwork materials. Edges and corners usually are matched carefully as to size so that the pattern will be consistent throughout the work.

138

SOFT PARCHEESI BOARD.
Sas Colby. Mixed fabric patchwork
on satin in pure spectrum colors.
28 inches square.

THE BULL AND BEAR.
Harlene Schwartz. Patch-
work and stitchery with
mink and rabbit fur,
suede, leather, silk,
tweed, labels, grey
flannel, organdy, cotton,
and a button. 36 inches
high, 24 inches wide.

LEATHER PATCHWORK.
Bernice Bruzelius. Leather
shapes are carefully glued
together to simulate the patchwork effect that is shaped and
contained by an octagon.

139

PATCHWORK

ISLAND IN THE SUN.
Foster Marlow. Patchwork
is carefully hand-stitched in
shapes that tell a story.
COURTESY: ARTIST

THE RANCH.
Foster and Patricia Marlow.
Patchwork with stitchery in gold,
white, red, and blue.
COURTESY: ARTISTS

LUCERNE.
Foster Marlow. Patchwork
of red, white, and various
blues. Mr. Marlow finds
this simple storytelling
patchwork technique a
marvelous introduction
to a textile art form.
COURTESY: ARTIST

PATCHWORK WEAVING.
Ted Hallman. The interplay of fabrics and shapes indigenous to patchwork inspired the artist to create a patchwork weaving.
COURTESY: ARTIST

HEXAGONS.
Bernice Bruzelius. Using prequilted fabric, the artist carefully cut hexagons with a template and arranged them collage fashion. Then she glued them to a fabric backing. Although all the hexagons are the same size, their patterns and placement give them variety.

TABLE COVER
Sas Colby. Using a modern approach to patchwork, Sas Colby develops triangular and trapezoidal shapes intricately to create an organized yet slightly unstructured effect. The patchwork is set into a solid rectangle so that it may be used as a table cover *(below)*.

RED HOT.
Sas Colby. Patchwork banner of satins, velvets, and corduroy.

MOTHER KNOWS BEST.
(Detail). Anna M. Sunnergren. A wall quilt made of satins and velvets stitched together and quilted over thin sheets of urethane foam. 4 feet high, 5 feet wide.

padded work

quilting, trapunto, and soft sculpture

Padded work generally means that there are several layers of fabric—usually a top layer, a middle layer of a thick material, and a bottom lining layer. There are basically three traditional approaches to padded work, which actually is derived from quilting.

First, in English quilting all three layers are the same size, and these layers are held together by sewing. English quilting was used most often for bed quilts because the padded fabric provided warmth and weight.

The second approach to padded work is Italian quilting, which consists of easily recognizable parallel lines made with running or back stitches on *two* pieces of fabric sewn together. The back lining fabric is slit, and the stuffing is pushed in between the top layer and the backing. Consequently, the finished work consists of both flat and stuffed areas.

The third technique, called trapunto is also an Italian version of padded work. Two layers of fabric are used as in Italian

QUILT (Nineteenth-century American).
First the entire surface was quilted; then each square was
appliquéd with a different design, no two squares are
exactly alike.
COURTESY: THE ART INSTITUTE OF CHICAGO

quilting, but the design is not restricted to parallel lines. Therefore, the trapunto technique lends itself more readily to contemporary quilting than do other quilting techniques.

However, padded work today goes beyond quilting methods. In fact, some artists may never have heard of trapunto. Linda Vetter, for example, developed her padded pictures simply to give greater dimension to her delicate textile paintings. Anna Sunnergren's wall hangings combine velvets and silks for rich color and texture.

Fabrics selected for the top layer of a work depend on the final presentation that the artist visualizes. Works based on traditional techniques rely heavily on the use of lightweight, semitransparent fabrics with a rich visual surface that changes with the padding and lighting. These materials include silks, satins, sateens, velvets, wet-look synthetic fabrics, shantungs and moire satins,

WALL HANGING.
(Detail). Joan Michaels Paque. Red and black satin is shaped by means of the Italian quilting and trapunto techniques. 108 inches high, 36 inches wide.
PHOTO: HENRY PAQUE

and dacron and cotton voiles that have a sheen and shimmering quality adaptable to quilting.

The stuffing for padded work may be cotton matting, dacron batting, spun polyester, kapok, or thin sheets of urethane foam. Backing materials and methods preferred for completing works differ according to the artist. Elsa Brown first uses a backing of lightweight nylon net basted to the back of the quilt top. She bastes top surface, padding, and netting together in a grid to hold it while working. Then with a darning foot on the sewing machine she freely "draws" the design on the right side of the quilt top through the layers. After it has been stitched, the quilt is turned wrong side up; the nylon net is slit in the center of each area to be padded; and cotton or dacron batting is pushed into these areas. Each slit is sewn closed by hand. A final lining of cotton, muslin, or other closely woven material is placed on the right side of the fabric and sewn together at the edges in the

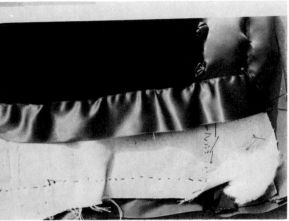

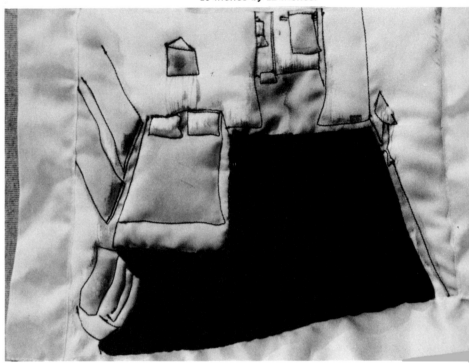

ROOM SCENE.
Linda Vetter. Red velvet and lightly painted silk.
Materials are stitched together in three layers. The
painting and machine sewing outline the design. About
10 inches by 12 inches.

ROOM SCENE.
(Detail). This photo
illustrates how the layers
are put together. The top
fabric is a closely woven
piece of duck with a layer
of cotton basted to it.
After the sewing had been
completed, the extra fabric
and cotton were trimmed,
the piece was padded, and
a lining was sewn onto the
back.

same manner as a huge pillowcase. Then the piece is turned
right side out, and the backing is tacked to the padded areas;
the opening is stitched closed by hand.

Modern padded forms go beyond adaptations of quilting
methods, and these techniques are easily recognized in the
accompanying examples. Padded work may be used in conjunction
with the other techniques illustrated throughout this book and
is an interesting point of departure for the art you create from
fibers and fabrics.

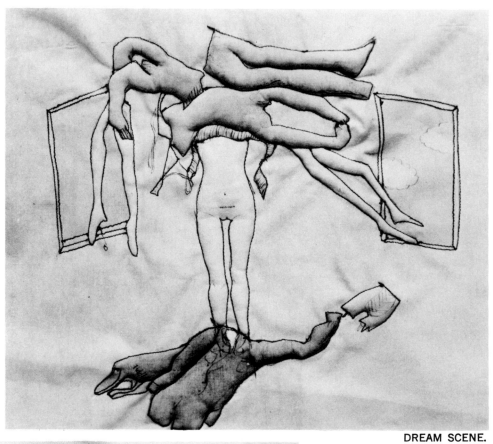

DREAM SCENE.
Linda Vetter. A variation of the
trapunto technique.

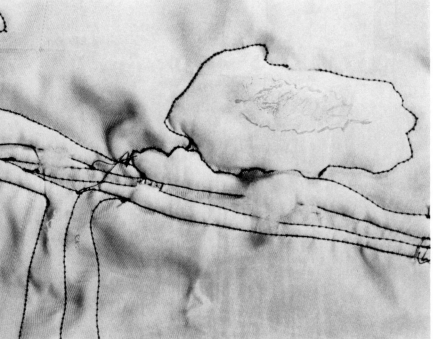

Linda Vetter sews her design on
two layers of fabric. The backing
fabric is slit slightly, and dacron
or cotton padding is stuffed in
with a sharpened stick or knitting
needle. The slit is then stitched
closed, and the piece is lined on
the back. The result is padding
with a flat background.

149

UNTITLED.
Liz Mapelli. A metal frame is the basis for stuffed felt with vinyl and beadwork. The piece was sewn by hand.

COURTESY: ARTIST

THE CHAIR MAN.
Nell Sonnemann. A stuffed participational sculpture that permits the figure's position to be changed on a chair. Some machine appliqué. Total figure measures 6 feet, 2 inches.

COURTESY: ARTIST

VESTA ONE.
Elsa Brown. Trapunto
hanging. 24 inches long,
16 inches wide.
PHOTO: K. Y. FUNG

TRAPUNTO DOLL.
Elsa Brown. The limbs and body
are made in one piece; the back
is also stitched and stuffed.
PHOTO: K. Y. FUNG

MAINE ROCKS.
Anna M. Sunnergren. A red velvet vertical section at the left is
set off by a large yellow wool rectangle. The bottom shapes, made
of black velvet, gray wool, gold silk, and wool fringe, are padded
to different heights to simulate rocks.

COURTESY: ARTIST

THE FINDING OF THE CROSS *(opposite page)*.
Nell Sonnemann. Solid and printed textured wools,
metallic embroidered silk, nylon, synthetics, and textured
cottons. *The fabrics are tiered vertically in four depth
levels. The hanging portions are mounted on four strips
attached to a panel of mirrored plexiglass.*

COURTESY: ARTIST

PADDED WORK

SOFT SCULPTURE II.
Evelyn Svec Ward. Hot pink
and black fiber sculpture on
a wood pedestal. Stitching
and cut work. Although no
actual padding was used, a soft
sculpture was achieved by
manipulation of the fibers and
fabrics. 13½ inches high, 13
inches wide.
COURTESY: ARTIST

STUFFED FORMS.
Virginia Tiffany. Styrofoam
shapes are covered and designed
with stitchery for a soft
sculptural hanging.

*PHOTOGRAPHED AT
ART INDEPENDENT,
LAKE GENEVA, WISCONSIN*

CAPE WITH HANDS *(right)*.
Sas Colby. Velvets with silk and satin appliqué, gold cording, and brass bells. Trapunto-stuffed sculpture forms and appliqué result in an art form that has been developed into an item that can be both practical and decorative. For wear the stuffed silk arms would be removed.
COURTESY: ARTIST

CAPE FOR A BLITHE SPIRIT
(bottom left and right).
(Front and back). Sas Colby. Velvet with silk lining, satin appliqué, fringe, wrapping, and bells.
COURTESY: ARTIST

PADDED WORK

TRAPUNTO HANGING.
Elsa Brown. White on white velvet. Trapunto enables you to develop design freely. Various portraits are "drawn" with the sewing machine on the top layer of the fabric, which has a layer of netting under it. The netting is slit, and the appropriate areas are stuffed and resewn. The entire piece is then lined on the back.

PHOTO: K. Y. FUNG

QUILTED STITCHERY.
Esther Robinson. A piece of fabric that has been carefully designed with the batik technique is quilted. The edging includes stitchery and beading. The entire piece is mounted on a textured backing and framed.

156

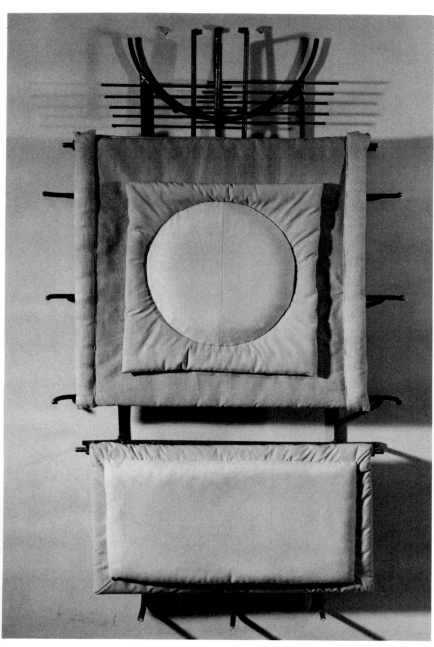

LUNAR FRAME.
Jeanne Boardman Knorr. Sculpture
fabric collage on a steel frame. 63
inches high, 36 inches wide.

COLLECTION: MRS. DEVORAH SHERMAN,
WINNETKA, ILLINOIS

VALENTINE.
Wilcke Smith. Black blanket wool padded and stitched with
colorful yarns. Hanks of heavily textured yarn are looped
and coiled in an arabesque of three shades of red.

COURTESY: ARTIST

157

IF.
Anna M. Sunnergren. Felt and satin letter shapes are padded with foam
and suspended from the hem at the top. The letter shapes are stitched
together, but they have negative areas between the shapes so that the
backing shows through. The shapes can be lifted away from the white
satin backing.
COURTESY: ARTIST

158

FLORENTINA.
Elisabet Siewert-Miller.
Textile relief with padded
shapes. 45 inches in diameter.
PHOTO: NICKERSON

SUPPLY SOURCES

The following list is for your convenience in finding fibers and fabrics. Local crafts shops, needlework departments, yarn suppliers, and department stores may carry some supplies. Fabrics have not been listed because they are readily found. Consult the classified section in the telephone book for additional sources. In this listing no endorsement or responsibility is implied by the author. Charges listed are subject to change.

*assorted materials including beads, bells, feathers, etc.
**$.50 charge for samples
***$1.00 charge for samples

Fibers

BRIGGS & LITTLE'S WOOLEN MILL
York Mills, Harvey Station
New Brunswick, Canada

COLONIAL WOOLEN MILLS, INC.
6501 Barberton Avenue
Cleveland, Ohio 44102

COLUMBIA-MINERVA
295 Fifth Avenue
New York, New York
10016

**CONTESSA YARNS
P.O. Box 37
Lebanon, Connecticut
06249

**COUNTRYSIDE HANDWEAVERS
Box 1743, W. Elkhorn
Avenue
Estes Park, Colorado
80517

**CREATIVE HANDWEAVERS
P.O. Box 26480
Los Angeles, California
90026

FEAR'S NORTH SHORE HANDWEAVING
107 Central Street
Evanston, Illinois 60201

FILATURE LEMIEUX
St. Ephrem, Beauce,
Quebec, Canada

GREENTREE RANCH WOOLS
Route 2, P.O. Box 318
Loveland, Colorado 80537

*P. C. HERWIG
264 Clinton Street
Brooklyn, New York 11201

HOUSE OF YARNS & FABRICS
P.O. Box 98
Hampton, New Hampshire
03842

**SACHIYE JONES
2050 Friendly
Eugene, Oregon 97405

*KNIT & KNOT SHOP
2701 N. 21st Street
Tacoma, Washington
98406

LILY MILLS CO.
Dept HWH
Shelby, North Carolina
28150

**THE LOOMERY
210 1st Avenue S.
Seattle, Washington 98104

*MACRAMÉ & WEAVING
**SUPPLIES
63 E. Adams Street
Chicago, Illinois 60603

*JEANE MALSADA
**FASHION ARTS STUDIO
P.O. Box 28182
Atlanta, Georgia 30328

*THE MANNINGS
**R.D. 2
East Berlin, Pennsylvania
17316

**THE NIDDY NODDY
One Croton Point Avenue
Croton-on-Hudson,
New York 10520

**SHUTTLE CRAFT
P.O. Box 6041
Providence, Rhode Island
02904

**SILVER SHUTTLE
1301 35th Street N.W.
Washington, D.C. 20007

SPINNERIN YARNS
230 Fifth Avenue
New York, New York
10001

**TERLINGUA DESIGNS
4120 Rio Bravo
El Paso, Texas 79902

*THREE GABLES HOMECRAFTS
1825 Charleston Beach
Bremerton, Washington
98310

TRAIT TEX INDUSTRIES
6501 Barberton Avenue
Cleveland, Ohio 44102

TUXEDO YARN COMPANY
36-35 Main Street
Flushing, New York 11354

***THE UNIQUE
21½ East Bijou Street
Colorado Springs,
Colorado 80902

*WARP, WOOF & POTPOURRI
514 N. Lake Avenue
Pasadena, California 91104

*THE WEAVER'S LOFT
320 Blue Bell Road
Williamstown, New Jersey
08094

*WEAVING WORKSHOP
3324 N. Halsted
Chicago, Illinois 60657

YARN DEPOT
545 Sutter Street
San Francisco, California
94102

YARN MERCHANT
8533 Beverly Boulevard
Los Angeles, California
90048

YARN PRIMITIVES
P.O. Box 1013
Weston, Connecticut
06880

**YARNS OF WALLA WALLA
P.O. Box 372
Walla Walla, Washington
99362

General crafts

***DICK BLICK
P.O. Box 1267
Galesburg, Illinois 61401

*CREATIVE HANDS CO.
P.O. Box 11602
Pittsburgh, Pennsylvania
15228

ECONOMY HANDICRAFTS
47-13 Francis Lewis
    Boulevard
Flushing, New York 11361

INTERNATIONAL HANDCRAFT & SUPPLY
103 Lyndon Street
Hermosa Beach, California
90254

J. C. LARSON
7330 N. Clark
Chicago, Illinois 60626

NORTHWEST HANDCRAFT HOUSE
110 W. Esplanade
North Vancouver, British
    Columbia, Canada

SAX ARTS & CRAFTS
207 N. Milwaukee
Milwaukee, Wisconsin
53202

TRIARCO ARTS & CRAFTS
Dept. 5810, P.O. Box 106
Northfield, Illinois 60093

VANGUARD CRAFTS
2362 Nostrand Avenue
Brooklyn, New York 11210

Rugmaking backings, yarns, tools, frames
(Many fiber suppliers also carry rug yarns)

AMERICAN THREAD CO. AUNT LYDIA'S YARNS
90 Park Avenue
New York, New York
10016

BON BAZAR, LTD.
149 Waverly Place
New York, New York
10014

NORDEN PRODUCTS
P.O. Box 1
Glenview, Illinois

PATERNAYAN BROTHERS
312 E. 95th Street
New York, New York
10028

STUDIO WORKSHOP
35 S. Washington
Hinsdale, Illinois 60521

UTRECHT LINENS
33 35th Street
Brooklyn, New York

Miscellaneous specialty items

J. L. HAMMETT CO.
Braintree, Massachusetts
02184
Lyons, New York 14489
Union, New Jersey 07083
(Circular knitting frames)

**EARTHY ENDEAVORS
13441 Camellia Street
Whittier, California 90602
(Unusual ceramic beads, bars, etc.)

**SONDRA SAVAGE
425 Narcissus
Corona del Mar, California
92625
(Unusual stoneware beads)

INDEX

OTHER BOOKS BY DONA Z. MEILACH

Contemporary Art with Wood
Contemporary Leather
Contemporary Stone Sculpture
Creating Art from Anything
Creating with Plaster
Creative Carving
Macramé Accessories
Macramé: Creative Design in Knotting
Making Contemporary Rugs and Wall Hangings
Papercraft
Papier Maché Artistry
Printmaking
The Artist's Eye

Collage and Found Art
with Elvie Ten Hoor
Creative Stitchery
with Lee Erlin Snow
Direct Metal Sculpture
with Donald Seiden
Accent on Crafts

DATE DUE

JUL 1 5 '76		
NOV 1 '77		
MAR 2 7 1979		
OCT 2 0 1980		
APR 9 1993		